NO. 13
HERBERT
ROAD

'The greatest evils and the worst of crimes is poverty.'

George Bernard Shaw

*   *   *   *

This book is dedicated to the memory of my parents and to my brother, David.

No.13 Herbert Road

Tales of Growing Up in Small Heath, Birmingham

PETER DOHERTY

HiP
HISTORY INTO PRINT

First published by
History Into Print, 56 Alcester Road,
Studley, Warwickshire B80 7LG in 2015
www.history-into-print.com

ISBN: 978-1-85858-349-5

A Cataloguing in Publication Record
for this title is available from the British Library.

Typeset in Haarlemmer
Printed and bound in Great Britain
by 4edge Ltd.

ACKNOWLEDGEMENTS

I would like to thank Honey and Luke for their patience, belief and encouragement. My sister Sheila whose memory is still as sharp as ever. My niece Judith, who started me off on this journey into my past and without whom I would never have written this book. I would also like to thank everyone who is mentioned, I have fond memories of you all and our adventures, I hope you remember it the way I do. I have removed surnames to protect the innocent!

BIOGRAPHY

Peter Doherty was born in 1939 in the Small Heath area of Birmingham. He grew up next door to one of the most over populated streets in the country towards the end of the Second World War.

He started his working life in Birmingham as a carpenter, but he held many jobs in the early days working on building sites, digging trenches, steel fixing, bricklaying and also working down the coal mines. He worked in the plastic moulding shops at Lucas and for British Rail, cleaning steam engines. He was a vacuum salesman, a roofer, an errand boy, a furniture removal man and worked in restaurants washing up.

Eventually he left Birmingham and trained as a professional actor winning a scholarship to drama school. He worked for many years in Repertory Theatre, in all parts of the country and for many years in fringe theatre. He has appeared in several TV commercials and acted in and produced several plays.

He went on to start his own building and decorating business, which he ran for many years.

No. 13 HERBERT ROAD

The Bombing

In 1940 I was a babe in my mother's arms, looking up at the stars with air raid sirens screeching in the background. She carried me to the air raid shelter in the cellars of the Greenway Pub, which was situated on the corner of the Coventry Road and Cattle Road, opposite St. Andrews, home of The Blues football team, who I would later support and still do to this very day.

But that of course would be in the future, I first had to survive the bombing raid, which thankfully I did. In fact I survived seventy-six more. What I remember and is still lodged in my memory is the people singing to keep their spirits up in the cellars of the Greenway Pub.

I don't remember much about the war, only being woken up and looking out of the window of my mother's bedroom and watching the people outside building a bonfire in the middle of the street. Later I would join in the fun and merriment, with the dancing and singing and the fireworks. The war was over and it was 1945, I was five and a half years of age.

We grew up playing on the bombsites, looking for ancient buried treasure. We found coins, metal plates, kettles, knives, forks and all sorts of paraphernalia, little realising at the time, they had only been lying there for a couple of years. Some of the bombsites were left with just the shell of a house still standing, some were left with only half the house remaining and some were completely flattened to just a pile of rubble. But we loved them. It was the first place we headed for, although we were warned they were dangerous to play on. We were kids and didn't know any better.

The bombsites were our adventure playgrounds and boy we had plenty of them.

Large Families

We were a large family, three boys and three girls. But not as large as the family who lived opposite, the Cattleys. I remember my mom saying when she was younger she had seen a photograph in the local paper of a man and his family, twenty of them or thereabouts. Little did she realise at the time that she would spend a great deal of her life living opposite them.

I played with Freddy and John, my elder sister Peggy played with the older children. They had the biggest house in Herbert Road, my mother said it was the Park House many years before. I think it was the only house in the road with a bathroom, everyone else had a tin bath hanging on the wall outside, to be filled with boiling water from the kettle in front of the fire.

When I was still very small, before my younger brothers and sisters arrived, Peggy and I used to go over there and have our bath. One day when we were at the Cattleys the air raid sirens went off, it was a daylight raid so we all huddled around Mrs Cattley in the kitchen. She said "Don't worry, there's nothing to be scared of," we didn't get scared until we saw the panic on her face. Then suddenly the all clear came and we went back to normal.

Freddy was the youngest and he was a couple of years older than me, then John a couple of years more, the older ones had already flown the nest so I never knew them. I used to say to Freddy, "Can you name all your brothers and sisters?" "Yes," he would say and off he would go, "Albert, Charlie, Bessie, Jimmy, Cathleen, Colin, Eunice, John…" and so on. I used to lose count after about ten.

My mother never really forgave Freddy for telling me Father Christmas didn't exist. I was there years later when the council moved them to a smaller house on the new Chelmsley Wood Estate, Freddy and his mom and dad. I went to visit them in their new little house, you could hardly move for furniture. It was rather a poignant moment. Sadly I never saw them again.

Outside Lavatory

We had an outside toilet, no hot water and no electricity. I can't remember when the electricity was first installed, suddenly it was there and compared to the gas mantle it was like Blackpool Illuminations. Before, when the gas mantle burnt out, we would dash to the shops to purchase a new one. Sometimes we would damage it in transit, much to our mother's dismay. Nothing was cheap. Gaslight was restricted to downstairs, we would always take a candle to bed and I can still remember the feeling of hot wax dripping on the back of my hand.

The lead pipes in the lavatory would freeze up and burst, but the tap in the house never did. It wasn't just one year, it was every year but we coped with it. It was par for the course, what we never had, we never missed.

Bonfires

Apart from Christmas, Bonfire Night was the biggest night of the year. Weeks before November 5th we would start collecting wood and cardboard, anything that would burn. We would rip out timbers from the bombed out buildings, stripping them almost bare and go around the shops asking for old wooden or cardboard boxes. A couple of days before the big night, we would start to build a bonfire on the waste ground. It was organised by us kids, most of the parents would join in after the pubs had closed. We would make a Guy Fawkes and stick him in a pram, then wheel him around the streets asking people to give a penny for the guy. Sometimes one of the smaller kids would be dressed up and stuck in the pram, I did it once and I didn't like it, but I had little choice.

The sheer excitement of waiting for Bonfire Night made us hyperventilate. They were halcyon days, the kids would bring their own fireworks, if they were lucky enough to have some. Oh, the excitement of watching a Catherine Wheel spinning (which only lasted about ten seconds), throwing jumping jacks and bangers and the occasional rocket, which flew no higher than the rooftops. Putting potatoes in the fire to bake them and by the time you managed to retrieve them, they would usually be burned to a crisp. The fire was so big you could hardly get near it and the older folks would play music and start dancing. It was wonderful, sometimes the fire would still be smouldering next morning.

I can't ever remember it raining on Bonfire Night, it was as if the Gods were on our side, making sure the kids enjoyed themselves (which of course we did). We did it for years. When they redeveloped the waste ground we retreated to our backyard and the fires became smaller, but were still great fun and we still organised them ourselves.

Today is different, it seems to be children's parents who do all the organising.

An Old Lady's Request

One Bonfire Night, after we moved it to our communal backyard and I must have been in my late teens, we were preparing the bonfire and getting everything ready for the evening, when this little old lady appeared. I knew her because she lived in Herbert Road, in one of the back-to-back houses. She was a nice old lady, she always said hello, whereas some of the other older people thought we were a nuisance. I would occasionally see her pop into the Regent Pub to have a glass of stout. I was surprised to see her suddenly appear in our backyard. She asked me if I would do her a favour. Of course I said yes. She told me she had some important papers to burn and could she bring them round tonight for me to dispose of them for her? Bring whatever you want, I said, and we will burn them for you. She enquired what time the bonfire started and after I told her she left saying "I will see you then."

I didn't think any more about it until she appeared again later. She produced this bag containing letters and photographs and handed them to me so I could burn them. I asked her if she was sure this was what she wanted. "Yes," she replied. It felt strange to see all those old photos curling up in the fire and disappearing forever. All the years those photos had been treasured, how many times had she looked at them? How many times had she read those important papers she had kept safe until now, all disappearing in the blink of an eye?

She left before I had finished burning them, making me promise to complete the job, which I did but I could not help feeling a little sad and perplexed by it all. I had the feeling I was doing something important. I didn't know how old she was, to us kids a person's actual age didn't matter, you were old and that was it. I may have now reached her age, I may even be older! She sort of hinted to me that her time was running out and she wanted to put her house in order. Today it all makes sense to me. Maybe it's the way we have been conditioned through our lives, we like to tidy up after ourselves. Maybe we are more private than we think we are, or maybe we're just protecting ourselves. Why didn't she use her own fire? She must have had one, there was no central heating back then and it was winter after all. Perhaps she just couldn't bear to do it herself.

No.13 Herbert Road

Our house at number 13 Herbert Road consisted of a front room, a back room and a scullery where mom cooked and there was a tap which was our only supply of water. It had two bedrooms upstairs, later on we would open up the loft and create another bedroom, which was luxury. Until we opened the loft, all the kids shared the same bedroom. I was still sharing a double bed with my two brothers into my early twenties. David was three years younger and Tony two years younger than David, we were all big boys and it was a little squashed to say the least.

The other double bed housed my two sisters, Sheila and Carol. Sheila was two years younger than Tony and Carol was two years younger than Sheila. By then my big sister had married and left home. Later I would leave, then David would marry and leave and then Tony would marry and leave.

Somewhere along the line my gran, my mother's mother, arrived and lived with us. We all lived on top of each other, nobody seemed to have their own space and consequently fights would break out amongst us boys. The bigger we grew the worse the fights got, no prisoners taken. How difficult it must have been for mom and gran.

The only heating came from burning coal, coke or wood in the fire grate, along with anything we could get our hands on. The larger the family became, the poorer we became, no hand-outs in those days! The rent was the most important thing, pay your rent or go to the workhouse, the dread that hung over most families. To think that our parents lived through two world wars and still had to live with this horror hovering over them, not forgetting the cold war. It affected our parents more than it affected us, we never lived through what they had to endure.

More Herbert Road

At 13 Herbert Road in Small Heath we had a small backyard, leading onto a large communal backyard we shared with our neighbours. One house to the left and two more to the right, the other side backed onto the shops on the Coventry Road, which consisted of a florist, tobacco shop, green grocer's, a cake shop and a butcher's shop. The rest was just a bombsite where six houses were flattened along with the shops, which was visible from our back window.

My mother said that when the buildings were hit, the power of the blast blew out all of our windows. Luckily we were all in the air raid shelter, except for our dad who was in his second home, the pub at the bottom of the road. The blast must have flipped the bed over because when we were allowed to return home after the all clear was given, we found my father fast asleep under the bed snoring, with the bed on top of him. There were no windows left in the house.

Our small backyard consisted of a lavatory and a small area, which mom turned into a miniature garden. She had a border running around the edge with blue and white lobelia and a beautiful array of summer flowers all grown from seed. Mom would plant the seeds and wait for them to grow, first would come the shoots, then the stems, then the buds and then the flowers. Magic. Not bad for someone who had never had a garden before.

Bomb Shelter

The bomb shelter was in the communal backyard when I was growing up, it would have been built at the start of the Second World War. It was a re-enforced concrete, brick built air raid shelter with steel blast doors, designed to withstand a direct hit from a German bomb. Compared to an Anderson shelter, which was corrugated steel covered in soil at the bottom of the back garden, it was more like a concrete bunker. The inside was dark, dank and full of rubbish. Nobody ever ventured inside, we looked into it and teased each other, but as far as I can remember nobody ever braved the interior, it was as you might say, surplus to requirements. People chose to use the cellars of the Greenway Pub instead, they must have felt safer and more secure there. To us kids the inside of the shelter may have been redundant, however, the outside was perfect to play on. As soon as I was big enough to climb onto the flat concrete roof, it became my new playground. When the summer holidays came round, so would the other kids and we would spend most of the day there, we loved it. Our parents never seemed to mind, at least it wasn't falling down like the bombsites we played on.

Sometime in the mid to late fifties, the builders arrived and removed it. It did not go easily, as it was undoubtedly well-constructed, but we were left with a much larger space to play in. We could play football or cricket, you name it we played it, the bomb shelter that was never used for the purpose it was built for was never really missed, I did well to remember it.

My mother told me that my big sister Peggy, at the age of no more than six or seven years old, on leaving school at the end of the day would head for the Greenway Pub. This was not to join dad in a drinking bout, but to take her place in the queue, to reserve positions for herself, mom, gran and baby me in the cellar. Mom would stoke up the fire at home, making sure it was warm and glowing, she would then relieve Peggy in the queue, giving her a break so she could warm herself and have her supper. Then back in the queue Peggy would have to go. Mom said she did it and never grumbled.

A Miracle

A couple of hundred yards up the road from where we lived was a bombsite which had been partially cleared, but leaving the shell of one house still standing. It was as if someone had peeled the skin away leaving the heart of it exposed. Some local men had pulled down the section of the buildings deemed too dangerous to be left standing, making it safe to play on. Although our parents warned us not to, we chose to ignore their advice, we would have been only five or six at the time. Scrambling over the exposed floor joists and clambering up the broken staircase, the bigger boys jumping over the holes in the floor, daring us to do the same. Somebody pointed out this one particular brick, which was slightly loose with half of it hanging out. The bigger boys told us not to touch it, if it was removed the whole house would fall down. We believed them and stayed well clear of it. That brick was the foundation of the house, the whole building revolved around it. I did wonder what it was doing half way up the wall and why it was loose. The big boys could touch it, but not us, they knew best so we listened to them. One day after playing in there, for how long I can't possibly remember with a couple of other kids my age, we left the house and were barely ten yards away, when suddenly we heard this rumbling followed a deafening noise which gave us the fright of our lives. We watched in shock and horror, as the building collapsed in on itself. By the time the dust had settled, half the inhabitants of the street had appeared, some of them dragging us away, telling us how lucky we were not to have been killed, and "that's what happens when you play in dangerous and derelict buildings".

Once we got over the shock of it, we started to see the funny side. It was a big fright for our parents, but we couldn't see what all the fuss was about. We weren't dead, we were still alive! When I was young, I thought like many kids that I was immortal, indestructible so I couldn't possibly die because I was the one person that will live forever! As young kids we had no concept of the fragility of life.

Maybe it was a miracle. We were close to death and never really aware of it. I think most people in their lives have a brush with death and are not always conscious of it. I did wonder how that brick became dislodged. The local council arrived and cleared the site up, leaving us with a piece of waste ground. So the destruction of our playhouse enabled us to have our first football pitch!

The Coke Yard

The winter would always be the most difficult time for us. Poverty, according to George Bernard Shaw, is one of the greatest of evils and worst of crimes. When I first read that I tended to agree with him. Poverty really kicked in when you could not afford to heat your home. Trying to keep warm in Herbert Road during the very harsh winters of the forties and fifties as we were growing up, was a great worry for our mother. We had a fire grate in all the four rooms, but everything revolved around the one lit fire in the living room. It was difficult enough to find fuel for one fire, the other fireplaces spent most of their lives unused, surplus to requirement. Coal was a luxury.

I was born in the front room of that house, as were my brothers and sisters, except my eldest sister Peggy who was born in the flats by St. Andrews Football Ground. I spent the first twenty-three years of my life living there. Maybe it happened when I was too young to remember but I cannot for the life of me ever remember seeing the coal man delivering coal to us. Now that would have been a luxury.

Unfortunately for us boys we had to go to the coke yard to collect our ration of a half-hundredweight of coke, which would have been considerably cheaper than having it delivered. The coke yard was about two miles away, but that was not the problem, the challenge was negotiating Kingston Hill. Every time we went there the road would be covered in snow and ice and be very slippery, going down the hill was a bit of a laugh, we just jumped into the pram and slid down. The problem would be pushing the pram back up the hill with the weight of the coke in it. The pavement was a no go area, owing to the fact that it was covered in ice, so traffic allowing we would use the middle of the road. Dangerous to say the least. Gloves, what were they? Socks were our gloves, but even if we had socks without holes in them our hands still froze. Try pushing a big heavy pram full of coke up a steep hill on an icy cold day with your hands in your pockets. Even if you arrived at the coke yard two hours before they opened, the queue would already be half way around the block. Once the yard did open it would still be another hour's wait before you arrived at the serving station. When you went into the yard you were met with a cacophony of noise, there were huge piles of coke and men busy shovelling it into the scuttles. After weighing it they would then tip it into your sack, if you were lucky enough to have one, otherwise it went straight into your pram spilling precious lumps of coke onto the floor. Then you were quickly ushered out to make room for the next pram, cart, barrow or whatever receptacle people could lay their hands on. When the coke ran out the gates would be closed so some people just had to turn round and trundle back home empty handed. This was the reason people started queuing early for fear of missing out.

With our coke safe and secure inside the pram, which by the way was all rusted up having spent most of its life outside in all weathers, we headed for home. From the gates of the yard it was virtually all up a dreaded steep hill. By the time we arrived home we were cold, tired and knackered. Our motivation was the thought of sitting by a nice cosy warm fire, working out how we could make the fuel last a week, before we were at it again. Thank god in those days we had long summers.

So we had just one fire and we were always jostling for position around it. There were three doors leading from that room, one to the front room, one to the scullery and one to the cellar where we kept the coke and gas meter, which was also accessible from a grate on the front pavement. When it became extremely cold, mom would make a fire upstairs, funds permitting and at Christmas time in the front room. Someone was always shouting, "Close that door!", "We're losing all the heat!", "You must have been born in a barn!".

Ironically Tony would later get a part time job working for Joe the coalman.

The Pawn Shop

Sunday was a very special day. It was the day we all dressed up, it was the day when families sat down and dined together. It was also a day when the shops were closed and when a calm settled over Brum and probably most places in the country. People seemed to move at a slower pace, speak in quieter voices with less traffic on the roads and fewer people on the streets. It was a day like no other day of the week. It was a day that made you hate Mondays, it was a day you never wanted to end, you savoured every last drop of it knowing you had to rise early on Monday morning and go to work or to school. Either way it wasn't something you were looking forward to.

The Pawn Shop played an important part in our lives. There was a certain pride amongst the working classes, as for most people in those days, and the thought of going to the Pawn Shop and meeting somebody you knew was beyond mortifying. Although inevitably it did happen to me on one occasion, we both stood there pretending the other one didn't exist and when we met each other later nothing was ever mentioned, but I was a little relieved to know that we were not the only family pawning our clothes. Every time you went there the place appeared empty, much to your relief. Maybe people were hiding round the corner waiting for others to vacate the shop because my little sister Carol told me Sheila would keep watch outside, then give her the nod when it was all clear and then she would sneak in. Although the shop was on the main Coventry Road the entrance was conveniently situated up the side street away from the prying eyes of others. You did all your business in the back of the shop.

The two most important days for visiting this establishment were Mondays for pawning and Saturdays for retrieving. Borrow on Monday, payback on payday. Everything was on tic, that's the way we lived, because Sunday was dressing up day and walking out day. When lunchtime arrived everybody retired to their homes, to sit down as a family and have what we would call Sunday Dinner. The one meal that brought you all together, well it did in our house. The leftovers from lunch were served up for supper, cold meat with pickled onions or pickled cabbage, sometimes with pickled beetroot and occasionally as a special treat piccalilli, lovely.

There is no stigma attached to the pawn shop today. The difference being people will quite happily say I'm off to the pawn shop, or I'll meet you in the pawn shop. Those three brass balls hanging outside have made a welcome return, which reminds me of my mother's joke: Why is a pawnbroker the smallest person in the world? Because he is the only man that can stand under his own balls!

The Lights Back On

Mom told me that before the war if you went into the centre of Birmingham all the shops were lit up, it was wonderful she said, streetlights on the main road! That was something I was looking forward to when the war ended. To think people had been in the dark for all those years with the blackout. Through the bombing we had shutters on the windows at night, it was against the law to allow any form of light to spill out of your house or building during the blitz so most people had blinds or heavy curtains.

So when the war ended, crowds of people would gather on the corner of Herbert Road and Coventry Road, just outside the bus garage, waiting for the street lights to come back on. It seemed like an eternity, there's nothing worse than waiting around when you're a kid. It all turned out to be a false alarm, so we all trundled back home, only to return the following evening. After another long wait, it finally happened. Wow! The streetlights were back on! A great cheer went up. It wasn't exactly Blackpool Illuminations but it certainly made people happy. Maybe it symbolised the coming of a new dawn, tomorrow would be a brighter day.

We would gather there again at the same spot a few years later, this time it would be to say goodbye to the tram. The good old open top deck tram, had become surplus to requirement. Out with the old in with the new. We all cheered and clapped, as it disappeared into the bus garage, only to make way for the new trolley bus. Those wonderful old trams, I think there's some talk of them making a comeback.

Ration Books

Ration books were essential, you couldn't buy a pound of sugar without them and you even had a coupon for sweets or a penny bag of waste, which was just dust from the bottom of the sweet jar. I can see all the kids' faces in the shop window, pointing and licking their lips. It was the same with the cake shop, only the cakes weren't rationed, but they were still unattainable.

I used to think if I became rich, I would live on cream buns and ice cream soda pop. Unfortunately it came down to a penny's worth of stale doughnuts, nothing went to waste in those days. When sweet rationing ended, I think every shop in the country must have sold out in one day.

We may have been short on rations and at times things were a little hard, but we were happy, the reason being there were always plenty of kids to play with. We played in the streets, on the bombsites and in the park. If you fell out with somebody, there was always someone else to play with. We played football, cricket, rounders, hopscotch, Johnny Knocker and hide and seek. When your mother stood on the front door step and called "It's time for bed!" you pleaded for just ten more minutes…

Best Friends

We all had lots of best friends. My first best friend was a boy named Brian, I can remember us sitting on the pavement saying we would both go to the same school, we must have been about four years old. We ended up going to different schools, Brian was Church of England and I was Catholic. But religion was not an obstacle to friendship, it was never mentioned and we all played together. Oh, the pleasure when the bombsite was cleared to create a kind of football pitch, where we played all day until it became dark.

The summer holidays lasted forever and we played every day except Sunday. Dribbling became the fashion, nobody passed the ball and if you did you'd never see it again. Later down the line, they developed the waste ground so we moved to the parks. By then, we were teenagers playing with kids from other streets. We formed football teams and joined a league. What I wouldn't give to play today!

Of course every kid in the area supported Birmingham City, it must have been in the late forties when I first stood on the terraces of St. Andrews. I still go to the occasional game with my brother Tony and his grandson, my great nephew Harry. He's like us now, committed. You can change your supermarket but you can't change your football team. Good luck Harry! I hope you have better luck than we had.

The FA Cup Final 1956

The Blues have had their moments, like reaching the FA Cup Final in 1956 when they reached the final playing all their games away from home (that must have been a first). Brian and I went to all the away games, which enabled us to get tickets for the final on the 5th May. What a moment that was, I ran down Herbert Road telling everybody.

At the semi-final at Hillsborough, where we beat Sunderland 3-0, The Blues supporters start singing "Keep Right On to the End of the Road" which became our anthem. The Blues sang years before any other clubs even thought of it. These days it's more like a chant.

When the final whistle went there was a pitch invasion. Brian dodged a Copper and got onto the pitch, I failed. The following Saturday the picture was all over the front page of the Birmingham Program and there was Brian larger than life. Great.

Going to London was a great adventure in those days, but it turned out to be disappointing when we lost. Their goalkeeper Bert Trautmann broke his neck, we all knew he was in trouble when the final whistle went and our keeper, the great Gil Merrick, ran the whole length of the pitch to comfort him. It was a great spontaneous moment of sportsmanship.

When we finally arrived home, to the great relief of our parents, my mother provided the *Birmingham Argus*, which was the local sports paper and there I was on the front page, I am the kid with his mouth wide open.

Football

There was a Brian moment in the fifth round of the FA Cup. We were playing the Baggies (West Bromwich Albion) at The Hawthorns on a cold, icy day on a frozen pitch. We were winning one-nil thanks to Peter Murphy's second-half goal and they were pressing for an equaliser. With minutes to go they had a corner. Ader Griffiths, the Albion winger, came dashing up to take the corner. Brian jumped up onto the pitch to retrieve the ball, Griffiths ran back to the corner flag, expecting Brian to throw the ball in. Instead Brian walked slowly towards him (picture a packed ground with all the supporters on the edge of the pitch and the Albion player screaming for the ball, thinking Brian was an Albion supporter, little did he know!). Brian seemed to hand Griffiths the ball and as he stretched out to grab it Brian booted it over everybody's heads right to the back of the stands, much to the delight of the thousands of Blues fans. I wonder how much Brian played a part in the Blues victory that day.

Cycle Speedway

Brian was my best friend for years and later on became my brother David's best friend. He was a naughty boy, clever, but naughty and always playing practical jokes. The last time I saw him after many years was on the sad occasion of David's funeral. David died at the age of forty-seven, it was a great shock and a sad loss for all of us, but I will talk about him later. My sister Peggy said "Brian it's so lovely to see you again after all these years." "That's funny," he replied, "the last time you saw me you told me to clear off!"

Brian as a kid was heavily involved in cycle speedway and just recently my sister Sheila sent me a clipping from a newspaper about Brian winning some award for reintroducing cycle speedway to the youth of today. There was a photo of him, he was a dead ringer for his dad!

We never see him these days, but our family still talk about him.

An Accident

Life did not go by without its knocks and setbacks for our parents, especially our mom who never seemed to stop working. Trying to keep us clothed and fed, she worked full time and part time, as well as running the house. People talk about super moms, well we certainly had one. Plus she had to cope with our problems.

One day I had a very nasty accident, breaking my leg in several places. My mom was working in the Regent Pub at the time as a barmaid and a cleaner, when she heard screaming, not realising it was coming from me. The kids in the street went round all the houses collecting comics for me, how my mother and big sister managed to haul those comics to the Queen Elizabeth Hospital I will never know. It is the same hospital that houses our wounded soldiers today.

The Holy Family

The Holy Family School stood on the corner of the Coventry Road and Oldknow Road, next to The Holy Family Church. On the other side of the church was the Singer Motor Works, which disappeared many years ago. All my brothers and sisters, including myself attended The Holy Family School, in fact it was the first school we ever attended.

I am unable to recall the event, due to my tender years, but apparently one day my big sister was told she would not be attending school that day, due to the fact that the school had been bombed by the Germans, I believe she was a little disappointed! If it had been me I would have cheered, the thought, or just the idea of no school would have made most kids cheer.

There were two schools situated close to The Holy Family, both were Church of England. St. Benedict's was named after the road it was on and on the other side of the Coventry Road was Oldknow Junior School, which was also named after the road it was on and stood about two hundred yards behind The Holy Family. Because the Catholic school was reduced to a pile of rubble it was decided by the powers that be, that we would share with the two schools. As infants we would go to The Holy Family at St. Benedict's and when we became juniors, we would go to The Holy Family at Oldknow Road.

A couple of years before I left to go to the senior school at St. Michael's, the rubble that was The Holy Family would rise like a phoenix out of the ashes, into a brand new school. I actually helped the school move back into their new premises, well it was better than attending class. Wow! We had our school back, no more sharing. We starting playing sports, I played in the first football team, I certainly enjoyed that. On my first day attending infant school my mother escorted me, then after that, my sister. Once I had mastered the complexity of going backwards and forwards to school, I was left to my own devices and escorted myself. I would leave through the back door, cross the backyard, go down the back entry, over the Coventry Road, jump on the bus and go to school. I was still only five years of age. It would be the same with my brother David, my brother Tony and my sisters Sheila and Carol. We would all make our own way to school before we reached the age of six. How things have changed!

After we moved into the new school they decided to start a football team, which I was desperate to be part of. They asked for a show of hands if you were interested in playing and I put my hand up, but nothing happened even though I was at the front I was ignored. They picked the first eleven, then they picked the second eleven. The idea was the two teams would play against each other, giving them the chance to assess the players and select the best eleven. I gave up and put my hand down when I wasn't picked for either team.

Just when I thought it was all done and dusted and my big chance had gone, they realised they were short of a goalkeeper for the second team. So I quickly put my hand up again and to my great relief I was finally chosen. They had little choice, mine was the only hand that was raised. I think they picked the bigger and healthier looking boys first, I know I was on the small side. It wasn't until I reached my late teens that I suddenly shot up, by the time I was twenty-one I was taller than most of the kids in the street.

The teachers got it right, in my first match we were thrashed six-nil, after all that I had conceded all six goals. As I was trundling off the pitch dejected, with my head bowed and feeling sorry for myself, to my surprise and sheer delight I was patted on the back and told that I had a great game. I was even happier still when I was chosen to play in goal for the newly formed team. Thus started my amateur football career. Before the season was over I was playing in the outfield.

Education

When my time at The Holy Family School came to an end I was about eleven years of age and it was time to move on to senior school, St. Michael's in Digbeth. From being a big boy in a small junior school, I became a small boy in a big senior school. I was a little apprehensive on my first day, but there were a couple of familiar looking faces from The Holy Family School that I recognised, who had left before me. Walking into the school and seeing the high glass cabinet full of sporting trophies, I was awe struck, I knew I was in big school. Most of the students' surnames were either Irish or Italian.

There were three class forms: A for the clever ones, B for middling ones and C for the "duffers"! I was assigned to the B form. I was so relieved I wasn't with the "duffers" but I knew A was beyond me, so I was happy. The classes consisted of about forty-five to fifty pupils. My biggest fear was coming last, at the bottom of the class. I never did come last, there was always somebody dumber than me, I was always in the mid-forties, but never last.

The second year was going to be good, we were going to have the legendary Mr Nicholson – the most popular teacher in the school. On arriving to start my second year, to my horror, I was assigned to C form, which was taken by the science teacher Mr Saunders, who was a nice man and a good teacher. I've always remembered the first and only class I ever had with him, he was talking about going to the moon and if it was possible to get there. He said they would need a fuel tank the size of Birmingham twenty miles deep and that was only to get there. How would they get back? The only other way would be to invent a new kind of fuel. That one class must have sparked my interest in space travel as I later followed the Apollo programme and watched the moon landings. After the lesson I was informed by Mr Saunders that I was in the wrong class, I should be in B form with Mr Nicholson, so I hadn't been demoted after all. This made me determined to try harder and do better. At the end of the year, when Mr Nicholson read out the results putting me in seventh place I could not believe it, I was sure they must have made a mistake, they were my best results ever. I never reached those heights again but Mr Nicholson was moved up to take the fourth year which was great news, I was to have another year with him, I can't ever remember playing truant when I was in his class!

It was a great sporting school. I represented it at football, cricket, athletics and boxing. For sport I would mark it ten out of ten, academically zero, although we had some good teachers: Mr Nicholson, Mr Harper (better known as Daddy Harper), Mr Saunders, Mr Parker and the Head Master Mr McCoy. All I can say is they did their best with me. My brothers would later go to the same school and Tony would become Birmingham Schoolboy Boxing Champion for his weight.

That really was the extent of my education. At the time I really didn't think education was that important. It wasn't a reflection on the school, as I said, they did their best with me.

Holiday

I remember going on my first holiday when I would have been about seven years of age. We were going to stay with dad's sister in Cheshire for a week. The excitement of the holiday started the moment we left the house and jumped on the No. 58 bus into town, then climbed into the steam train at New Street Station. When I think about it now, mom would have been carrying Sheila who was just a baby, Tony would have been about two and a half, David a couple of years older and of course me too. Quite a handful for mom.

Once we settled into our compartment and the train was on its way, she allowed me to venture up and down the corridors and explore the train. Poking my head out of the window when the train was at full speed, I felt the wind blowing in my face, forcing me to screw up my eyes before I dared to open them again. I think the word is exhilaration. It's something I loved doing for years – I think most kids did.

When the train pulled into the station, there was our Aunty Lizzy waiting for us. We were on holiday and it felt special. As far as I can recall that was the first and only holiday we ever had as kids. But mom did manage to take us on lots of day trips over the years, to various seaside resorts.

My aunt and uncle had adopted two children, a boy about my age and a girl a bit younger, who were technically our cousins. We all played happily together. They lived in a bungalow in a leafy road with a back garden, leading onto a field with cows grazing in it. There was a wood at the far end and a stream where people fished, paradise! A far cry from Herbert Road. I can still see myself playing with David in the fields amongst the cows and cowpats and venturing to the edge of the wood.

I remember going into Chester city centre with mom and baby Sheila, we went into Woolworths leaving Sheila outside in the pram. When we emerged from the shop a crowd of people had gathered round my sister, making comments on how beautiful a baby she was, which of course pleased my mother. Can you imagine leaving an unattended pram with a baby in it today?

Street Parties

Street parties have been lodged in my memory for years, I loved them. Though there were plenty of kids in the street, we didn't go into others peoples' homes. We all knew where each other lived, but only crossed the threshold on rare and special occasions. Our lives tended to unfold on the streets. That's why street parties were so magical. The first party I remember was for VE Day (Victory in Europe). We sat down at tables that seemed to go on forever, laid out with jelly, trifles, ice cream, soda pop and all sorts of luxury items. The party lasted all day, then at night there were bonfires, music, dancing and the Hokey Cokey.

This was shortly followed by VJ Day (Victory in Japan). As the day of the street party got closer and closer, sadly it became apparent that for me this was one party I would miss out on, due to the fact I had chicken pox. I was coming up to my sixth birthday and my mother was concerned I would be missing out and felt sorry for me, she told me I would have my own party. She started making jelly and blancmange, telling me everything was going to be okay. I was a little too young at the time to take it all on board, I wasn't too worried and my mother seemed more concerned than me. When the big day arrived, just as we were about to tuck into our jelly and jam, there was a knock on the front door, when she opened it she was greeted by one of the bigger boys on the street. He said he had come to collect Peter and to be quick because the party was about to start. She was thrilled for me as the big boy grabbed me by the hand and we both ran up the street to where all the tables were all laid out and there was a seat already waiting for me. When I look back on it they must have been discussing my situation, maybe they realised my illness had run its course and it was time I joined in.

After that several years later, we celebrated the Queen's Coronation. The committee was mostly made up of women, they would gather on the waste ground to plan the party and make collections around peoples' homes. For the big day the weather forecast predicted rain so Bastock's, the local undertakers, came to the rescue allowing us to use their covered, disused yard with just a few old glass Victorian coffins scattered around! Not to be daunted by such trivial things, the committee stormed in with brooms and mops, transforming the place with tables, benches, flags, a piano and even a stage, which I would later perform on. Trying to get me onto the stage was a little difficult, but getting me off it was virtually impossible, as I sang my way through my repertoire of Frankie Lane songs.

The party lasted for a couple of days and when the weather improved we ventured outside for more bonfires, more dancing and more Hokey Cokey. Yes, I loved those street parties but that was the last one I ever attended. Life moves on.

Toy Soldiers

I still remember when I very small, maybe five or six, I was sitting with my friend Freddy on his doorstep with a couple of bigger boys, playing with his toy soldiers. I am unable to recall who they belonged to, were they Freddy's or one of his older brothers? Maybe they were passed down through the family. In those early days he must have been the only kid in the street who possessed such treasures. I think they were made of lead, I believe back then most toy soldiers were made of lead.

All of them were carefully lined up ready for action, those soldiers must have taken part in many battles and even wars, some of them were carrying broken weapons, some of them were missing arms, some of them without legs could hardly stand up. There were a couple of them with their heads missing and still they were bravely marching into battle. The army truck, with a wheel missing, was still trundling along heading towards the enemy. I think I must have been there for hours, because darkness began creeping in upon us and then the call went up signaling to me it was bedtime. Reluctantly I made my departure but the battle was still raging on.

Oh the blissful innocence of childhood!

Goal Posts

The bombsite to our right was re-built sometime in the fifties. It was an extension of the butcher's shop, where they made sausages and smoked the bacon. It also became a delivery depot for the rest of their other outlets. My brother David would later get a job driving their delivery van, he was well liked by the family who owned the butchers. The side of the new building cut across the end of the communal backyard, giving us a nice new brick wall which we painted goal posts onto. Kicking the ball against that wall gave me great pleasure for years. I kicked the ball with my right foot and when it returned I kicked it back with my left foot. That wall helped me become a two-footed player.

Years later when everybody had left or moved on and the houses were demolished, the only building left was the butcher's factory, it remained for several years before they built the new estate. Until then you could see the goal posts when you exited the Coventry Road entrance of St. Andrews. A sports journalist friend of mine once came up to Birmingham to report on a game for a National Newspaper. I mentioned my goal posts to him and he was curious to see them, but he failed to locate them. I think the new estate gobbled them up.

Barmy Harry

"Barmy Harry!" That was the shout that went up when he turned the corner from Coventry Road into Herbert Road, all the kids yelled, "It's Barmy Harry!" The moment he saw us and heard us, he started performing. He wore a top hat and often carried a walking stick. He would do crazy things like stop and salute, remove his shirt and wrap it around his stick and wave it above his head as he marched up the middle of the road. We would all fall in and march behind him, laughing and chanting his name. When he reached the entry which led to the back-to-back house where he lived he would stop, salute, doff his hat and take his leave with us still laughing and cheering. He never really talked to us, he would just appear, perform and then disappear. Who needed computer games when you had Barmy Harry?

Everybody liked him, even our parents. My mother told me that before the war, he was a very respectable postman. Sadly, his house was bombed, killing his wife and family, he survived but he was never the same again. My last real memory of him was years later, when we were teenagers. He was quietly walking up the road, it was a very windy day and his hat blew off. We managed to retrieve it for him and he insisted on rewarding us by giving us a penny. We knew he was poor but he insisted and we didn't want to offend him. Somebody said he was off to the library to read the newspapers. I can still see him now walking down the road, holding his hat on in a comical and exaggerated way, until he disappeared out of sight.

Long Trousers

All the boys wore short trousers and socks that came up to your knees and which were always falling down. Your mother was constantly telling you to pull your socks up. The magic age for long trousers was thirteen, the year you became a teenager. My first pair of long trousers were heavy, worsted, hardwearing and very, very itchy. They were so long they came up to my chest and braces were the order of the day, having a belt around my chest would have looked decidedly silly. They also had very sharp creases, which were of paramount importance. I stood on a chair to put them on, I couldn't bear the thought of my turn-ups dragging on the floor. Then at night, I placed them over the back of a chair to keep the creases in, a habit I kept up for years. I don't know how long I had those trousers, I would have outgrown them before they wore out!

Tricks on Bikes

Suddenly everybody's dream was to get a bicycle. Brian and my brother David somehow managed to acquire a tandem with a little motor attached to it. Not only was David big and strong but he was also mechanically minded. They performed lots of tricks for the amusement of everybody, David would sit on the handlebars with one hand on the throttle and Brian would sit on his shoulders.

One summer's day they came flying down Herbert Road, overtaking a man on a bicycle who happened to be an off-duty Policeman. He was so outraged that he arrested them and it all ended up in court. The Policeman stated that one boy was sitting on the handlebars with the other sitting on his shoulders, with their arms outstretched as they flew past him. Brian spoke up and said this was impossible, due to the fact that somebody had to have their hand on the throttle, otherwise the bike wouldn't be passing anyone. They got off with a light fine, to the annoyance of the Policeman and with a write-up in the local paper saying this was no mean feat even for a circus performer! They had the last laugh and I believe Brian still has the newspaper cutting.

Milkman

Another incident involved the local Milkman. He had a huge carthorse and milk wagon, which must have weighed a ton with heavy glass bottles in metal crates piled up to the roof, that horse certainly earned its oats. Picture the Milkman with his head stuck in his order book, when the tandem came gliding by. The boy up front gave him a slap on the back of his head, as he jumped up with shock the one behind nicked a bottle of milk. I never witnessed it, but knowing the Milkman, he would be jumping up and down in fury, even more so when they repeated the prank thirty minutes later. I still laugh when I think about it.

Taking to the Road

My bicycle became a big part of my life and in the late fifties and early sixties I practically lived on it. Every Sunday we would cycle to Stratford upon Avon or Evesham and all the surrounding country villages. In the summer we might cycle up to a hundred miles, the more miles we did the stronger we became. With my friend Peter, we even cycled to Blackpool and once to Oxford and back in the same day, about 130 miles. We were getting pretty good but we never actually joined a cycle club, I don't know why, we seemed to be happy with just the two of us.

Even keeping track of the Tour De France in the newspapers, I was a mad keen cyclist right up to the time I left Birmingham in 1963. After that, I never really cycled again. Bikes sort of disappeared and it would be decades before they made a real comeback. People's dreams shifted towards cars or as that great American writer James Baldwin referred to them "glorified pieces of tin". It wouldn't bother me if I never drove a car again. If I could afford it, I would have a chauffeur. It's wonderful to see that the bike is back, cyclists just need to learn the Highway Code!

Culture

We did have some culture in our lives, our mother made sure of that. She always managed to take us to the theatre. It wasn't heavy drama, more light entertainment, though it was theatre nevertheless, with the excitement of watching people perform live on stage. My big sister Peggy and I would go on a Thursday every time a new show would come to the

Birmingham Hippodrome. I was still very young, my sister being five years older than me, so I would leave school early, jump on a bus into town and take my place in the queue and wait for my sister to arrive. Nine pence we paid to sit up in the Gods. I would gasp in awe every time I would enter that magical Victorian theatre. We kept going for years, but as time went on and the family increased, it seemed to peter out. It probably became too much of an expense for my mother, how she ever afforded it in the first place is a mystery. We still managed to go but less frequently. Later on my sister would become an avid theatregoer visiting the Birmingham Rep and the Royal Shakespeare Theatre in Stratford upon Avon, plus trips to the West End. By the time her two daughters had grown up and flown the nest, they must have seen every Classical play from Ibsen, Strindberg and Shakespeare, to Shaw and Brecht, Chekhov and Moliere and everything else in-between. She saw many of the great performers and even the future greats, including myself.

I became an actor.

Out of Work

When I left school I worked for a few years then it all seemed to stop. I began to hate it, being stuck in a factory all day. There is nothing wrong with working in a factory, people do it and they enjoy it but I couldn't. My mind was somewhere else. It was hard being out of work and failing to provide for your keep when everybody else worked in those days. If you didn't you were ostracized, looked down upon as a sort of outcast and branded as being lazy.

I wanted something else, but I didn't know what it was. I craved something better although I had no way of knowing how to achieve it. I did a variety of jobs from night shift work to cleaning steam engines and training to be a train driver, lots of kids would have loved it, but I hated it. I even did a stint working down the coal mine! The work didn't put me off, it was just that my mind was somewhere else. As I approached my twenties, things became considerably worse and this lasted until I left Birmingham, when I was about 23. I have to say those were the unhappiest years of my life.

Somewhere in my late teens, my thoughts turned to the theatre. To anyone else that would have seemed ridiculous as the theatre was all about voice and diction. My diction never existed, I couldn't sound my h's or my t's, it was 'here' not 'ere' and it was 'thought' not 'fought'! And on top of that, I had a terrible stutter. Not a stammer, a full-blown stutter. An affliction I had for years, even on a bus I had trouble stating my fare, I could never get it out. People would often finish my sentences for me, which made me feel worse, but at least it hurried things on a bit. I wasn't born with it, I acquired it by watching and aping an older boy in the street.

When I finally managed to overcome it and I was working in the theatre, I often wondered what I would do if I were offered a part that required a stutter. I have always been quite cheerful, happy and a bit of a joke teller as well as very optimistic, but those years were hurtful. Not only for me but also for my family, especially my mom. Things are different today, you can live off the dole and there is no real stigma or crime for not working. It was like being on permanent holiday by the seaside with it raining every day and having no money to spend in the amusement arcades. For the working man holidays were few and far between. If Christmas and Boxing Day fell on a weekend, you were back at work on Monday. Maybe I was ahead of my time, being out of work!

The Three R's

My reading ability was years behind other kids and my spelling never really existed, I still struggle today. I can't quite remember when I got into reading but I do remember reading a book about King Arthur and the Knights of the Round Table and then joining the library. Those wonderful Victorian red bricked buildings also housed the swimming baths where we learnt to swim and the Turkish and washing baths, where we used to go and soak in a huge tub of hot soapy water. In the summer time long queues formed, waiting to get into the swimming pool.

I loved going to the library. One day I thought I'd read all of those books, I never did of course but I read quite a few. Most of the books back then went over my head, although I still struggled through them. Somehow I managed to acquire a recording of John Gielgud reading Shakespeare's Sonnets, which I played over and over again, I still do a pretty good Gielgud impersonation. That was my first introduction into Shakespeare, then when I could afford it a trip to the Birmingham Rep. I then read Cedric Hardwicke's *A Victorian in Orbit* in which he talked about the Rep and all the great actors that performed there, the list is very long. If I had said to anyone back then that I wanted to be an actor, I'm sure they would have laughed. So I never mentioned it.

The Workhouse

The workhouse, to think it still existed in my lifetime. It was either pay your rent or go to the workhouse. It was like the sword of Damocles hanging over our parents' heads, fighting for your country and then being dragged to the workhouse.

When I was still at junior school a family of kids moved in next door, we hardly ever saw them, they scarcely left the house until one morning I heard people yelling. The backyard was piled high with their furniture and the mother of the kids was running around the yard screaming. She had a knife in her hand and was threatening to do harm to her children. My mother tried to calm her down but it was chaotic and frightening. Men in suits (the bailiffs) were removing the kids, they were all going to the workhouse. What happened to them, God knows. I could tell my mother and big sister were in shock and we were all shaking in terror.

Recently I have seen a couple of buildings that used to be workhouses turned into smart, trendy apartments. What a difference 50 years make.

War Stories

In the mid-fifties when I started working in the carpenter's shop, there was a bloke there who did his National Service in Germany. He told me this story: One day he was sitting in the barber's shop when the German gentleman who was cutting his hair, asked him whereabouts in England he came from.

"Birmingham," he replied.

"I've been there," said the barber.

"You have?" asked the bloke.

"Yes," he said, "Twice. On bombing raids." It's a funny old world.

A Bet on the Side

Having a bet on the horses or the dogs was illegal when I was growing up. Betting shops never existed, a man would stand on the corner usually wearing an overcoat and you would surreptitiously hand him your bet as you walked past which he would slip into his coat pocket. Your bet consisted of a piece of paper with the money wrapped inside, the name of the horse or horses you were betting on and your moniker. The moniker was of course your identification. My dad's was always Tony after my brother, my mom's was always Sheila Anne after my sister and my gran's was granddad's army number (he had died before most of us were born). If my dad won, he would walk up to the man on the corner and say "Tony" and he would slip him his winnings.

They could only afford to bet a few shillings at a time and if they were lucky and won, it was only a few shillings more. On very, very rare occasions they might win a couple of pounds. People bet because it gave them hope, a sort of dream of winning money. People bet today and of course people are still poor, but somehow it was a different kind of poverty then. There are a lot more things around today and they are a lot easier to get your hands on.

Another New Arrival

One morning I was about to leave for school when my mother who was mopping the floor, suddenly felt very dizzy. She said she must sit down. She was pregnant. "Off you go," she said, "You'll be late for school." When I came back home the next-door neighbour, Mrs Bridgeman, greeted me. She led me through the heavy curtains which divided the living room from the front room and there was my mother sitting up in bed with a baby in her arms. The midwife said "This is your baby sister." She then asked my mother, "What are you going to call her?" My mother looked at me and said, "Peter can name her." As the midwife looked at me, she must have realised by my worried and perplexed expression that I was dumbstruck. She quickly came to my rescue and reminding us it was Christmas time. "Why don't you call her Carol?" At that moment I perked up and named my little sister Carol.

Naming a baby today can take months of sorting through hundreds of names and when finally settling on one, often the spelling is then changed.

The Festival of Britain

I arrived at school one morning, which of course I hated, the only consolation was I was in the classroom with my favourite teacher of all time, Mr Nicholson. If I learnt anything at school, it was because of Mr Nicholson and I thank him for that. When he handed out the milk in little glass bottles, he never exactly handed them out he threw them out. "Doherty!" he would say, then he would lob the bottle at me. Everybody in its path would duck and I would stand there, hands at the ready, just like playing cricket. The shout would go up "Catch it!" and I did. Everybody loved it. It never filtered through to the MCC that the best slip fielders in the country were at St. Michael's in Digbeth, Birmingham!

This particular morning was special because Mr Nicholson made an announcement that we were all going to The Festival of Britain. I think most of us cheered but wondered what is The Festival of Britain? "It is in London," he said. "London?" we gasped. London to us was like going to the moon. The Festival of Britain is something that seems to have been forgotten about and now, of course, I realise how important it was. After years of austerity it was time to make a change, look to the future and show the world what we were capable of, a new dawn to give people hope.

We were going to London "Wow!" The expectation of going there made me hyperventilate. My mother walked for miles looking for sweets to give me for my trip, that's what mothers do. She failed. Rationing was over and the sweet shops were empty. She felt really bad about it but I didn't mind I was going to London! The meeting place was outside the school, everybody was early and I mean, everybody. There were three coaches waiting for us, one was brand new state of the art, I still remember its name 'The Dollar Princess'. That was the coach that I travelled on and even its name smacked of 'luxury'.

We arrived and going into the Dome of Discoveries, what a wonderful experience. But unfortunately, that's where things started to go wrong. I saw this big screen showing the solar system and planets orbiting the sun. I was fascinated by it. I had never seen anything like that before in my life. I don't know how long I stood there absorbed in it, but when I turned around the class I was with were no longer there, just throngs of people all massing about heading in different directions. I was lost. But I kept calm, knowing I would bump into them sooner or later. In fact I wasn't even bothered at all. I was too young and naive to realise the trouble I was causing.

A couple of hours must have passed before I finally bumped into them. We were all lined up in two's, a kid named McLaine and me were both situated at the front. He looked rather distressed. He was held responsible for me going missing and he had been beaten. I felt a little guilty but he never blamed me. Everybody was relieved, especially the teachers. The day ended happily and we all went back home to Brum.

The School Board Man

When my little brother Tony left school he started working for the Milkman on the Co-op milk round. As a job it was no great shakes but it was a job nevertheless and he loved it and the milkman he was assigned to loved him. Not only because of the speed at which he dispatched the milk, but also because of his ability to do all his bookwork. Tony was like our mother, good at sums and mathematics, it was his forte. In a different time, in a different place, who knows what he could have achieved? In the last couple of years of his education he moved schools, he wanted to be where his friends were. They liked to run wild, which suited my brother. Even though he was hardly ever there his marks were still good, especially maths. He lost a few marks for neatness otherwise he would have scored one hundred percent.

A few years later my mom, Tony and I were in the backyard when the school board man came strolling up the back entry. Tony's first reaction was to run and then he realised he had finished school three years earlier! I suppose old habits die-hard. The school board man said laughing "I haven't come for you I've come for the kids next door!" and he proceeded to tell my mother the Headmaster thought Tony was the brightest boy he ever taught.

Tony was going to work one morning, which was a good half an hour's walk down the back streets and through the viaducts in the dark, as milk men are early risers. They are clinking and placing milk bottles on peoples' doorsteps when everyone is tucked up in bed. The viaducts that Tony had to negotiate at five-thirty in the morning were dark and forbidding places, with water continually dripping down. On this particular morning Tony was dodging the water cascading down from the arches, when he came face to face with a man wielding an axe. Tony, quickly realizing he was about to be attacked, turned and scarpered with the man in pursuit. Luckily for him there was a row of houses just by the railway bridge and luckier still there was a light on in one of the houses and a woman standing on the doorstep. Tony headed straight for her. That woman turned out to be a lifesaver and they both piled into the house and bolted the door behind them.

Tony was very shaken and when he reported the incident to our mother she asked me if I would escort Tony to work the next morning, which of course I did. Tony never forgot it, he tells me from time to time what a hero I was. I often wondered what I would have done if it had been me being confronted by an axe wielding mad man!

Looking at Art

In my dark days of desperation and unemployment, I found great solace in frequent visits to the Birmingham Art Gallery and walking into that great building with all those great works of art and the collection of the Pre Raphaelites. It was a provincial gallery, but what a great collection of artwork! The museum which was attached to it, housed a stuffed Bengal Tiger in a glass case. I wonder if he is still there? Maybe he has escaped!

People tend to snub their noses at the mention of Birmingham, making disparaging remarks and terrible attempts at a Birmingham accent. They tend to forget that Birmingham was the workshop of the world manufacturing jewellery, silver, guns, motorbikes and motor cars. You name it Brum made it. Even the great Scottish engineer James Watt plied his wares in Brum.

Brum is awash with canals, if it was supplying the world then it had to transport the goods somehow. For years the canals were oily and uninviting places to go, we were told not to play by them because if you fell in you would drown in the grease and oil and junk that was tossed into them. Today they have been cleaned up, people enjoy strolling along them, there are bars, cafes and restaurants alongside. I wish they would have been like that when I was playing truant and out of work.

A Very Important Person

Mom, my big sister Peggy and I were standing on the corner of St. Benedicts Road and the Coventry Road, opposite The Holy Family School. David and Tony at the time would have only been babies and Sheila and Carol would arrive in the world a few years later. Mom had chosen a very good spot because the cavalcade of cars slowly came to a halt on the corner of St. Benedicts Road, before turning into the main Coventry Road.

The man we were all waiting to see was seated in the back of one of the open top cars, mom had often talked about him and how important he was. He must have been very important because there were thousands of people jostling for position just to catch a glimpse of him. There he was in the back of the stationary car, you could almost reach out and touch him. I can still see him now turning towards us raising his hand and giving his now famous two fingered victory sign. It was none other than the man himself, Winston Churchill.

Many years later I would meet and befriend his younger cousin Viscount Peter Churchill, but that is another story for another time.

Roy Rogers

I don't remember the exact date, but it must have been some time in the early fifties when Roy Rogers came to Brum. For us kids he was the biggest star in world. He arrived with his beautiful wife Dale Evans, also a film star and of course the most famous horse in the world Trigger. They were the personification of glamour, something we could look up at on the big screen in the cinema.

I think when I was a kid like most people in those days I practically lived in the cinema. Some were so posh it felt uplifting just to walk over the threshold. Every kid went to the cinema to see Roy Rogers. If the feature film was good then that was a bonus, but if it wasn't who cared? There was only one feature and that was Roy and now he was coming to Brum! Along with our parents and cousins, Margaret and Kenny, and a few thousand more Brummies we waited outside The Queen's Hotel, which is no longer there.

We must have been there a good couple of hours before they appeared Roy, Dale and Trigger. We were all packed in behind a barrier as they paraded up and down, waving and chatting to the crowd, then they walked back into the hotel. The crowds were still calling for them and they did not disappoint. The doors opened up on the hotel balcony and suddenly they appeared, even Trigger! The crowds were calling for Roy to sing and he did, the song was called 'Home on the Range'. Wonderful! But that wasn't the end of Roy, there was more to come...

Although I didn't know it at the time St. Michael's School was situated in Floodgate Street in Digbeth, just round the corner from the Bird's Custard House less than a hundred yards away. At lunchtime everybody was playing in the playground when some well informed kids said Roy Rogers was having lunch at the Custard House. Well the news spread like wild fire and within minutes practically the whole school headed towards the Custard House. We were all waiting outside when somebody came flying round the corner, shouting the whistle had just blown at school and lunchtime was over. A few filtered back but most of us stayed, it would mean the cane but who cared Roy was worth it! Can you imagine the look on the teacher's face when he went into the playground and there was nobody there!

Meanwhile back at the Custard House the doors opened and out came Roy and Dale, walking down the steps and smiling at us kids. After, we all scurried back to school, did we get the cane? No, I think caning the whole school was not an option!

Christmas

Christmas was always very special for everyone, including us. In our house it was all down to our mom and later on when she started work, my big sister Peggy helped buying Christmas presents and all the things that went with Christmas, the usual paraphernalia. Where was my father? You may well ask. Probably down the pub.

When we were still quite small, fear and dread hung over the house at Christmas time, especially for our mother who worried about his irrational behaviour. Would he come home on Christmas Eve drunk, full of hatred and bitterness, spoiling for a fight? Was he determined to ruin everything for us? Maybe, because to say that he never contributed is an understatement. I can't ever remember him buying anyone a

Christmas present, not even a Christmas card. It was the same with our birthdays, nothing. It all fell on the shoulders of our mother.

We hung paper trimmings from the ceiling, some left over from previous years and tinsel round the mirror. It brightened the room up, it was nice to look up and see it, and it was pleasing to the eye. We even had a small Christmas tree in the front room with coloured balls hanging from it and even more tinsel, with a fire burning in the grate.

We kids enjoyed Christmas in spite of our father. Even if he did knock the trimmings down with his crutch, we would soon put them back up again. When we awoke on Christmas morning, like all kids did at the crack of dawn, there on the floor placed neatly by the bed were our presents and our stockings hanging over the end of the bed. We would have an apple, an orange, a few nuts, a few sweets and a couple of pennies. We would be eating the contents of the stocking and at the same time, with great excitement, opening our presents and then we would go dashing into our parents' bedroom to show them.

Mom couldn't believe it either, she was as excited as we were!

Holes in Shoes

In the late forties, throughout the fifties and into the sixties when it snowed it stayed on the ground for weeks, sometimes months. Then it would thaw, freeze and snow again. I remember my feet being wet and uncomfortable with water seeping through the holes in my shoes. You tried filling the gaps with bits of lino or cardboard which was fine until it rained! Our dad was a cobbler so you would have thought he would have repaired them for us, that of course was wishful thinking. You had more chance of acquiring a bag of fresh cream buns than having your shoes repaired in our house.

The only pair of boots I had without holes in were my football boots. In those days they were made of thick leather with long leather studs. So what did my father always say? "Wear your football boots!" Can you imagine walking down the street and going to school in them! That's how much our dad cared, he wasn't going to spend his beer money on leather for our shoes, he even had his lath at home, his driver, his pairing knives, his boot hammer and various other tools. The reason being he would mend the neighbours' shoes at the weekend, it was extra beer money for him. I don't think any of the money filtered back into the upkeep of the house.

I used to watch him, I was always fascinated when he tossed all the tacks into his mouth, then picked them out at a rapid speed one at a time as he drove them into the shoes. He then finished them off with his boot hammer, followed by his special trick of spinning the hammer in his hand to amuse us. I never learned to put tacks into my mouth but I certainly learned to repair my own shoes and of course spin the hammer – a little trick I can still do to this very day.

Free Boots

There were plenty of times when things were very tough for us. I cannot remember if my mother applied for them or how she qualified for them, but qualify she did for free boots for me, somebody on high was giving them away. People were proud and they liked to earn their own money to buy their own things without accepting hand-outs, but because she was desperate she swallowed her pride so off we went to get the boots.

She was concerned I would not like the stamp on the side of the boot identifying it as being government supplied, I wasn't bothered boots were boots. Anyway it was stamped on the top part of the boot, conveniently covered by my turn-ups. We queued for hours in the freezing cold wind, but it was worth it, they were certainly worth waiting for. I remember I nailed metal studs into the soles, which enabled me to slide on them, also saving the wear and tear on the leather soles. Nobody ever said to me "those boots aren't shop bought!" They lasted until I grew out of them and they helped my mother at the same time. I sure did love those boots!

Dad

When my father was a young man he had his left leg amputated above the knee. My uncle Jim, dad's brother told me he had his leg in irons for years then gangrene set in and they had very little choice but to amputate. So my mother married a one legged man. Today you would say so what? But back in those days things were a little different, there was a certain stigma attached to 'cripples', people looked down on them and saw them as lesser human beings. The world today is finally catering for the disabled with the wonderful Paralympics and with pavements and buses designed for wheelchair users. More importantly, the way society views the disabled has changed for the better, they haven't changed we have. It has taken a long time but we are getting there.

My father's parents died when he was still very young. He was placed in an orphanage with his two brothers, then later on sent to a special school for invalids. The ethos of the establishment was to provide curative treatment and an elementary education, with instruction in learning a trade.

My father became a shoemaker, a trade that has almost disappeared, maybe because we are living in a disposable age.

Dad's younger brother Hubert obtained permission from the orphanage to emigrate to Canada and he was placed with a farmer in Carleton County, Ontario. Sometime later he moved on and became a gold miner. Dad often talked about his brother Hubert and my mother corresponded with him and his family. Photographs were exchanged, he had married and had two children, a boy about my age and a girl a little younger. Alas, time passes and you lose contact, dad never did see his brother again. I often wonder what happened to our cousins. Did they have children? Are they still alive? Some years ago a Canadian friend of mine was going back home to see his parents, who lived roughly in the same area. I asked him to look in the telephone directory for the name Doherty, so he did and his reply was yes, there were hundreds of them!

Dad had lots of brothers and sisters, dad being the second youngest of about 10 or 12 children, but we saw very little of them. I know there were several cousins who lived in different parts of the country who we never got to see.

My father worked all his life and always went straight to the pub after work. For years my mom dreaded him coming home drunk and later on so did we. What kind of life was that to live? We would later ask her how and why did she put up with it. "I did it for all of you," she would say.

As we grew up and became young men and dad was getting older, he quietened down. David was his least favourite son, though ironically it was David that looked after him when our mother died. He started his early life in a home and he dreaded the thought of ending up in one, so he spent the last days of his life living with and being looked after and cared for by David and his wife, Sheila. He was welcomed and made comfortable and I think he enjoyed it. My niece, Samantha, recently researched his early life, it was all very moving. He was a bitter and angry man and when drunk a bloody nightmare. But he was our dad and we loved him for it.

Gran

When we were kids at times life could be a little tough, but compared to our grandmother, it was like a walk in the park on a summer's day eating an ice cream. She started work when she was about 13 years of age. The amount of miles she would have to walk every day, back and forth to work, is enough to make you wince. She appeared ancient and was very thin but very upright and deceptively fit and strong. Maybe her fitness was down to all the miles she walked going to work every day when she was a teenager. She always seemed to be up on her feet, always on the go. She had very few luxuries in her life, maybe a bet on the horses, a little pinch of snuff which she kept concealed in her apron pocket to be taken when no one was watching and sucking the occasional humbug. She never indulged in the luxuries of drinking and smoking.

She told us a story of when she was a little girl and how she found a shilling in the street. She bent down to pretend to tie up her shoe laces, then when she felt no one was looking, she slipped it into her shoe. Then she ran all the way home. Of the 12 pence she had found, 10 pence was spent on a big slap up roast dinner for all her family and 2 pence for herself. A bob would go a long way in those days.

She lived for many years on her own in a back-to-back house, her husband who was considerably older, died before the Second World War had started. The only access to her house was down a dark alley, it consisted of two rooms, a scullery and an outside lavatory. She just lived in the one room, cooked on the fire and slept on the chaise longue. The older she got, the more vulnerable she became. When night fell, she would wedge the chaise longue against the door for safety. So mom suggested us kids would take turns sleeping with her, which of course we did. We didn't mind. At least it was a change of scenery.

When they opened up the loft space in Herbert Road creating a third bedroom, we boys moved up there and Gran moved in with us, sharing with the girls. She was a real character, strong willed and a little bit of a troublemaker, so teasing her was the order of the day. Her way of fighting back was to swear at us, I once asked mom if she had always sworn? "No," mom replied, "she never swore until she met your father, he taught her." It was almost impossible for him to form a sentence without using an expletive. When people came to the house, mom would say, "Mind your language, Tom." So he would change the word 'f**king' to 'p**king'. All my brothers and sisters and her other two grandchildren, our cousins Kenny and Margaret, can tell funny and amusing stories about Gran.

Sadly, one day in the late 1960s when she was walking down the Coventry Road, she slipped and fell. Somehow she managed to get back home and went straight to bed, never to leave it again. My little sister, Carol who spent a lot of time with her, told me she became frightened and was scared of dying. All this happened after I left home, for some reason I never came back for her funeral, for what reason I do not remember.

The Rubbish Dump

Just off Garrison Lane, almost facing St. Andrews Football Ground, tucked behind a row of houses, was a large patch of waste ground. If you walked across it you would eventually get to the railway, which I believe was the main express line out of Birmingham. The railway was not our intended destination, it was the 'rubbish dump' that would be our port of call. There were no plastic bags then, just loose rubbish dumped into metal dustbins, these dustbins would be collected by the dustmen and then emptied into a dustcart. Dustmen never wore gloves or masks then, they wore the dust instead. When they arrived at the rubbish dump to deposit the waste, they would be greeted by dozens of people ready to scavenge their way through other peoples' rubbish.

I don't ever recall finding anything of note, what I did find was the smell and the stench that emanated from those mounds of rubbish would limit my time of exploration. I didn't even know what I was looking for anyway. The grown-up scavengers were organised and appeared to know what they were looking for. How they found anything of use or value, only they would know but there must have been something in those bags that they slung over their shoulders, even if it was only a piece of rag to cover their faces, preventing the smell from permeating up their nostrils. But that is what you did if you had nothing.

Throwing Stones

When we were quite small, we tended to play with kids at our end of the street, we rarely ventured very far from our section of Herbert Road. It must have been the same with most kids in the area. Of course as we started to grow up the more adventurous we became and I started making friends with the kids from the top end of the road, I even ventured into the next road, Arthur Street which had even more kids in it than our road. I read somewhere, in the fifties it was the most heavily populated street in the country. At that time it was full of back-to-back houses, talk about sardines in a tin, in fact by the time I had reached my late teens I had more friends in Arthur Street than I had in Herbert Road.

Some kids lived in the remaining houses of what was left of Kingston Terrace but the bombing had flattened most of it. Our mother told us that our father had been sitting on the horse trough, drunk, outside the Greenway Pub and watched it go down. She said if the blast had been in the opposite direction he would have gone down with it. I think my father must have lived through the war in a haze of alcoholic intoxication. The houses that remained were at the far end of the Terrace, so for years people had to walk across the rubble to get to their homes. Kingston Terrace is now part of the Birmingham City Football Club's car park.

When you played on the bombsites there were always plenty of stones and broken slates, so throwing stones at kids from the other streets was a very popular pastime. These stones and broken bits of slate, for some reason or other, nearly always landed on top of my head, which would result in cutting it open and making it bleed profusely, then I would run home screaming with blood pouring down my face, frightening the life out of our mother. I have never shaved my head, but if I did it would be full of tiny scars and so would the heads of the other kids who indulged in the friendly game of stone throwing.

As we grew up we graduated from throwing stones against each other to playing football with each other.

Railway Children

There was a time when we were still very young when we used to play on the railway lines, not so much the lines, more the railway banks. The railway lines were out of bounds and playing on them was against the law. They were covered in long grass, with wild flowers and bushes and were fun to play on. The line cut across Kingston Hill, along Kingston Terrace and behind St. Andrews Football Ground, because of the bombing we had easy access to the railway line. The line was more of a slow freight line rather than an express passenger line. If you happened to be playing on the line when the train came, you were never in any danger as you could hear the train puffing and chugging with smoke belting out of it from miles away. You would scramble up and sit on the bank and wait for it to crawl by. At the speed it was going it seemed like an eternity. One day when I was sitting on the bank with another kid we saw this man come charging down the opposite bank shouting at us to stay where we were. Our first inclination was to run, but for some reason we were rooted to the spot, it was like being stuck in a car's headlights. The man turned out to be a plain clothes copper, who arrested us on the spot. There were lots of tears as he led us to our respective homes. We were summoned to appear in court to our parents' annoyance. They thought a good cuff round the ear would have sufficed. We were young and frightened and were given a ticking off in court and also fined half a crown (that was two and sixpence in old money).

A few years later when we were older and wiser we started playing on the railways again, ready to scarper whenever we saw anyone, copper or no copper. One summer's day we jumped over the fence in Kingston Terrace and to our shock and horror the whole side of the bank was on fire, so we hastily ran to the police station, which was situated just up the Coventry Road. They contacted the fire brigade who promptly came to the rescue. After putting out the fire, they thanked us telling us it could have been very dangerous. One day you are a naughty boy, the next you are a hero!

The first time I was in court I was terrified, the second time I was a spectator at David and Brian's bicycle debacle, which I thoroughly enjoyed. In fact over the years I would often go to the Law Courts in Birmingham and watch the various cases, I found it fascinating.

Many years later I would be called to do jury service at the Old Bailey. Thankfully it did not involve kids playing on the railway line, I think I know whose side I would have been on if it had. Whilst on duty at the Old Bailey, I bumped into a barrister friend who later became a judge and I loved listening to his stories.

Food on the Table

Although we were poor we never starved, mom made sure of that. Feeding six kids on a pittance wasn't easy and of course the larger we grew the larger our appetites became. Licking the plate clean in our house became very fashionable, much to our parents disgust. We grew up eating offal and the old man would say "not tripe again!" but I loved it. We would fight over the kidney from the rabbit until sadly myxomatosis ended all that, black pudding was wonderful, frying it is a desecration, just peel it and eat it.

Although we never starved we were always hungry. If you were lucky you could scrounge a thick slice of bread with lashings of butter and even more lashings of jam, otherwise it was bread and dripping. That would keep us happy for a few hours. Sunday was the day we would all sit down and eat mom's Sunday roast, it was rather special. Even the cat was fed with scraps under the table, no pet food in those days and no fat kids either, obesity didn't really exist.

Breaking Wind

It is extraordinary how your brain hoards everything away, to be triggered by seeing something or hearing something and out it pops, like a computer waiting for someone to touch the right key. This particular incident has popped out several times.

Breaking wind today is almost fashionable, you only have to turn on the TV and somebody is farting all over it. When I was a kid you only broke wind in front of other kids or when you were at home, never in company. Some people have claimed to never do it! If one did slip out you never owned up to it you just looked at somebody else.

Well on this one occasion I was sitting in the cinema with my mate Peter, half way down in the left hand aisle where there were a few empty seats. The rest of the cinema was more or less full. During a quiet moment in the film when everybody was absorbed in looking up at the screen, my mate suddenly broke wind. Up until that point in my life it was probably the loudest fart I had ever heard! Just as I was thinking how brave he was to do that in front of all these people he suddenly jumped up and pointed his finger at me and in a voice so loud it would have been a credit even to a town crier, shouted "You are disgusting!" Then he promptly walked away in disgust and sat in a seat a couple of rows behind.

I could feel the whole audience staring at me thinking I must be the most revolting person ever to enter this picture house, I just sat there but I wanted to shout out at the top of my voice "It wasn't me!"

The Living Room

When you entered through our front door in Herbert Road, you would walk into what was referred to as the front room which was hardly ever used, we had a couple of bits of furniture, a sideboard, a couple of easy chairs and later a settee with the odd framed photo on the wall and a couple of rugs. Because the room was hardly ever used it was permanently clean and tidy, the windows were always clean and so were the curtains. It was our best room. You passed through it to get to the living room, which was divided by a heavy curtain to keep the draft and cold at bay. Somebody was always calling out to either shut the door or draw the curtains, for some reason nobody ever remembered to.

The rooms were more or less square, the front room had a wooden floor situated over the cellar and the living room floor consisted of red quarry tiles some of which were cracked and misshapen with a rug placed between the couch and the fireplace. People referred to it as the hearth and to keep the floor clean you would have to get down on your hands and knees with a bowl of hot soapy water, a scrubbing brush and plenty of elbow grease. We had a pine table nestled between the window and the door to the scullery for eating on and as a storage place for our provisions. There was also a couch and a couple of easy chairs, plus a couple of wooden chairs around the table.

We only ever sat in dad's chair when he was out, it was positioned to the right of the fireplace, with the cellar door behind him and facing the window, which enabled him to keep a beady eye on the backyard. The fireplace was one of those old fashioned black grates with an arm you could pull out to hang the kettle or the cooking pot on over the fire and a couple of ovens either side which were very useful for keeping the food warm. Above the fireplace was the mantle shelf with a tasselled fringe around it and various knick-knacks and 'objets d'art', in the winter it was where the camphorated oil was kept ready to be rubbed on our chests when we had a cold or cough, of course not forgetting the cod liver oil which tasted disgusting. The scullery was attached to the living room, with a back door to the yard, outside lavatory and the back entry that led to the Coventry Road.

The so-called kitchen consisted of a long brown stone sink and the tap that of course was our only water supply, plus a draining board and a gas cooker. Later on mom would acquire a kitchen cabinet with a couple of drawers, cupboards and the middle section which you pulled down giving you a workspace. The place was dark and dank, mom worked by candlelight until the electricity arrived. She must have spent most of her life in that hole cooking and washing our clothes. Outside was the old mangle we used for wringing out the wet clothes by turning the handle. Mom said we were always clean and presentable when we left home but on our return we looked more like a chimney sweep's assistants.

Sometime at the end of the fifties or maybe at the start of the sixties the old fire grate was removed and replaced with a new modern one, they were all the rage, trendy and at first we loved it. The ceiling was also plastered and painted, before that it was embarrassing when people came in and looked up to see the holes in it and the laths hanging down where the old man had prodded it with his crutch telling us to keep quiet in the bedroom above, at some point some of it actually fell on his head. The tongue and groove panelling that went around the room to the height of the dado was a dark brown, in fact all the colours of the room were dark and dank, so when the ceiling was replaced by the council and re-painted white and the new modern grate installed we set about decorating it. The tongue and groove was painted a light bright colour, the walls were also re-papered with bright flowery paper. Most of the work was done by my brother-in-law Frank, my sister Peggy's husband, he was adept at decoration and carpentry. I also waded in myself to help and enjoyed doing it. When it was completed it looked like a palace, I couldn't get over it. I wanted the whole street to come and marvel at it.

Looking back now, that so called modern grate probably wasn't that special after all, the heat that emanated from it was the equivalent to a one bar fire, the modern fireplace was characterless and the only thing missing were the three ducks flying up the wall. That old black leaded grate had dominated the whole room, it was the main focal point and it had a multi-purpose use, not only did it heat up the room but you could also cook on it and even keep everything warm in the ovens. It had great character and was good to look at.

Mom's Singing

Mom was always singing around the house, I think it kept her spirits up. Her repertoire was endless and old fashioned, even then. When I am watching TV sometimes old tunes trigger something in my head and I start singing, even today I still know most of the words. The list would be too long to name them, I am tempted to pause and sing one right now!

Dad used to hum or whistle when he was at home. We never had the luxury of a piano, it's a pity because dad knew how to play and if they went into a pub and they had a piano he would start tickling the ivories. Where he learnt to play is a mystery. He could also play the mouth organ, the spoons and he used to put pennies between his fingers and click them together and make a tune. Maybe he learnt it when he was in the orphanage, he certainly was musical, but it is another case of what if?

The Rats

When I was very young we had our fair share of rats, mom said they came from the bombsites. I had no idea where they came from, but arrive they certainly did. They would always appear in the scullery but were never spotted in the living room. Maybe they never fancied their chances with the old man. They are the reason we always had a cat and all our cats were given the same name, Tiddles.

When mom came down in the morning she would often find dead rats in the scullery and I know of at least one Tiddles dying from a rat bite. I also remember one of them being poisoned by the neighbours, some people can be funny about cats. As we grew up the rats became less visible but we did have the odd mouse running across the floorboards in the bedroom at night as upstairs was out of bounds for the cats.

I am sure we were not the only house with rats, the whole of Brum must have been infested with them. From time to time the R.S.P.C.A. van would appear outside the Kingston Cinema on top of Kingston Hill, for the benefit of the locals and their pets and what's more it was free, if you wished you could always put a couple of pennies in the charity box and mom made sure we always did. The way they treated the animals with love and tender care left a lasting impression on me.

Knitting

Knitting played a big part in my mother's life, as it did with lots of women in those days. On the rare occasion when she had the chance to sit down she would start knitting. She collected patterns out of the *Woman's Own* magazine. She would buy a hank of wool, roll it into a ball, place it on her lap, take up her knitting needles and off she would go. I like to think she enjoyed it as a kind of relaxation and sort of therapy creating something, sometimes a pullover, a scarf, a cardigan and lovely woollen jumpers. I think they were called Fair Isle jumpers named after the place where the wool came from. There must have been thousands of kids walking around wearing Fair Isle jumpers.

Later on in her life she went to work at Lucas's, they had factories all over Birmingham. At some point in their lives most people in Birmingham worked there or had a family member who did, I know most of our family did including myself, something I will talk about later. The factories never closed, they operated around the clock and I know they looked after their workers, when people retired they organised day trips for them and Christmas parcels. Mom joined the committee and one of her jobs was to knit clothes for the kids' dolls for Christmas, a lot easier than knitting a pullover for grown boys!

The Chip Shop

Sometimes you wake up in the morning not really knowing what the day has in store for you, occasionally it's a nice surprise, a little treat maybe. This was one of those days.

Before I left for school, I would go into the scullery and put my mouth under the tap and gulp down the fresh cold water. In those days it came from the Elan Valley in Wales, it was beautiful, soft and delicious. I could never drink tea, so apart from the odd luxury bottle of pop I only ever really drank water.

Mom could not always afford school dinners, so she would give me sixpence to buy some chips for my lunch. There were always plenty of chippies around wherever you were. My favourite one was on the main road by the school, which had a table and benches where I would sit and scoff my chips. Unbeknown to me on this particular day, as I was heading into the chippy my mother came past on the bus and saw me. The chippy was situated at the bottom of the hill, just outside the Bull Ring opposite the police station. In the shop I was ordering my chips and as I was pulling the sixpence out of my pocket I suddenly dropped it. Could I find it? No. The woman behind the counter was becoming impatient and I was beginning to panic. To my complete surprise and delight my mother appeared like an apparition in the doorway "Don't worry," she said, "here's another sixpence for your dinner."

As I was eating my chips and talking to my mother, who was still looking at the floor wondering whatever had happened to that sixpence, she then turned to me and said "Have you looked inside your turn-ups?" No I had not, but when I did there it was, settled amongst the fluff. I offered it back to mom who said "Keep it, it's a little treat."

The Night Watchman

When they started the re-building of the bombsites, there was a man who guarded the sites, as well as the tools that were needed in the reconstruction. He was called the night watchman and at the end of the day, when the builders retired to the comforts of their own homes, the watchman retreated to his little hut on the building site. This particular bombsite was technically out of bounds (the correct word was 'No Trespassing'). So when we ventured near the night watchman would come charging out of his hut and chase us off. If he had asked us to leave instead of chasing us away, we probably would have gone and never returned, but chasing us away was like a red rag to a bull.

When we became bored in the evenings, a source of entertainment would be to taunt the night watchman and throwing stones on top of the corrugated roof of his hut usually brought a rapid response. Even though we knew he had very little chance of catching us, we would still run away, my mate Peter and I. We kept it going for months, I wonder how many miles he covered in pursuing us?

One Sunday morning Peter and I were walking down the Coventry Road in our best suits, when we came face to face with the night watchman. He would probably never have noticed us only our reactions gave us away. He could not believe his luck! There he was confronted with his tormentors, barely an arm's length away. There was a moment when we all froze, he didn't quite know what to do. We did, we turned and ran. We were lucky, the entry that led to our backyard was situated close by and so we headed straight for it, with the night watchman in hot pursuit.

We arrived in the backyard at the same time as my dad was coming out of the lavatory. He wanted to know what was going on, we replied "there's a man chasing us!" "What man?" he asked as the night watchman came flying round the corner coming face to face with my dad. By sheer co-incidence and unbeknown to me, he happened to be one of dad's drinking buddies. Well the embarrassed look that came across the night watchman's face and the strange noise that came out of his mouth! He said "Tom, I had no idea!" My dad demanded to know what his mate was doing chasing his son, he wasn't happy about it. "I am sorry Tom," he said, "I had no idea he was yours!" He was beside himself with mortification and he quickly reached inside his pocket and gave us some money. He backed away apologising, disappearing down the entry from where he had just appeared, with my dad shouting after him "You ought to be ashamed of yourself, a grown man chasing kids!" I think if we ever thought for one second that when we were finally captured we were going to be rewarded, we would have surrendered sooner!

Down the Pits

I have talked briefly about the different jobs I have had, I think I was so desperate to get a job I even applied to be a coal miner. It is something I have never really talked about, but I have nothing but admiration for those miners I worked with, I saw how hard they laboured and during the miners' strike in the 1980s I know whose side I was on. It was just that during that period of my life I was most unhappy. I know when my mom would get me up early in the morning I would jump on the bus to Birmingham with my sandwiches, then catch the train at New Street Station for Cannock, where I did my training. I remember staring vacantly out of the window, eating my banana sandwiches and by the time I got to Cannock I had scoffed the lot.

I found it difficult to absorb the information that was being given to me, I was in a daze and I felt I was walking through treacle. After my training I moved down to a place called Hamstead, just north of Birmingham, where I started life as a miner, working at the bottom of the pit uncoupling the coal trains. The work was very hard, you worked for about twenty minutes and then you would have your rest and then start again. The idea was to build up your strength so you could eventually work without resting. Then after a certain number of years, you would work your way up to the coalface.

One day while I was there somebody at the coalface was killed, so they set up a relay to carry the body out, as they approached the station where we were working, everybody stopped and formed a guard of honour. The thought hit me, if I was working hard to get to the coalface would this be my reward, ending up dead on a stretcher? Apart from feeling sorry for the miner and his family, the whole episode left me really disheartened.

I tried chewing tobacco like the other miners to keep my mouth moist with all the coal dust about, I never did take to it although I enjoyed the bit where you spat it out afterwards. I preferred taking snuff, I even enjoyed the sneezing afterwards as it cleared your head. It was my mind that needed clearing, I needed to get away and start my life somewhere else. I envied people who were happy in what they were doing. After several months I left the mines.

I have worked down the pits but I would never presume to call myself a coal miner, they are a very special breed.

National Service

National Service was something most young men dreaded. My only real knowledge was the information that filtered back from the boys who had already completed it. Eighteen years of age was the magic year you started National Service and it lasted for two years. So after spending the first years of your life hardly venturing out of your area, to be suddenly thrust into a situation where you were deposited in a part of the country you hardly knew existed, in the company of complete strangers, with strange sounding voices was a shock to the system to say the least! No more of your mother's home cooking, this was a completely different ball game.

Reveille at the crack of dawn, sleeping and sharing a billet with other boys, ironing and washing your own clothes, square bashing on the parade ground for weeks, polishing your boots so you could see your reflection in the toe caps clear enough to be able to comb your hair, constantly polishing buttons and keeping your uniform pristine, they said that it was endless. Not forgetting the tears and the homesickness. At that stage in your life two years was a long time, the one thing the boys all had in common was that they couldn't wait to get home. Consequently the boys who were waiting for the dreaded day to arrive were not exactly jumping up and down with joy. Some wag said "don't answer the door when they come calling". If you were serving an apprenticeship then twenty-one was the year you were given your marching orders. Having a trade must have been an advantage, I think the boys who served an apprenticeship were probably better off for it.

When you talk to those now who did National Service, like all things, they only remember the good times. There have been lots of debates about whether or not it should be re-instated but I imagine it would be a strain on the army to accommodate a whole nation of eighteen year olds! In some kind of perverse way I was looking forward to doing my

National Service, but alas it never came to pass. It was slowly phased out in the late fifties, to disappear forever. Those who were born in 1939 would be the last year of call up and if you were born in the last quarter of 1939, you would miss out. I was born on October 18th 1939 so I was saved by eighteen days, which my mother reminded me of often. If I had been born a few weeks earlier, I would have ended up on the parade ground.

Man in Chains

When I was still attending St. Michael's School in Digbeth, on Friday afternoons we would walk in a line of twos through the backstreets, winding our way around the factories and the back-to-back houses. Our destination was the Catholic Church where we would attend mass for the last hour of the day. The church was situated about ten minutes' walk from the Bull Ring and after mass that's where we would head for. The Bull Ring would be a hive of activity there was always something going on, after all it was the market area. There would be somebody on a soapbox ranting and raving, sometimes about the price of soapboxes!

But the real attraction for us was the man who was trussed up in a straightjacket and chains. The crowd would form a circle usually three or four deep around him and we would squeeze our way to the front to watch in awe as he wriggled his way free. Before he attempted to rid himself of his shackles, he would invite people to come forward to check and make sure the chains were secure, what you would call milking the crowd! Then he would roll around on the floor until he was free. After the performance he would take his bows to the cheering and clapping and then walk round the crowd with his cap in his hand collecting money for his endeavours. That would be our cue to disappear!

About a year ago I went to Stratford upon Avon with my brother Tony and his wife Janet. It was my first visit there for many years and after trolling round the shops for several hours we finally ended up in the actors' pub The Dirty Duck opposite the theatre. When we left the pub after oiling our vocal cords, we found ourselves heading towards the green and eventfully the river, when suddenly we heard a great cheer go up, followed by clapping. Tony, who was walking slightly ahead of Janet and I, had a better view than us and I called out to ask him what was going on. His witty reply was "I think it's much ado about nothing!" So like most people we headed towards the crowd in the centre of the green and low and behold there in the middle of the crowd was a man trussed up in a straightjacket and chains. I could not believe my eyes, I thought that kind of act had disappeared with the laced football. It was good old-fashioned entertainment, Shakespeare would have approved, I certainly did. I did not sneak away this time I waited for the hat to come round.

Food

I've already briefly mentioned food and although we never starved we were always hungry. Meat and two veg was our staple diet when we could afford it and we all survived and looked healthy for it. Rabbit served us pretty well, practically every shop on the Coventry Road had rabbits hanging outside. Rabbit stews, we had plenty of those with dumplings and pearl barley, I loved the dumplings. Did I love the pearl barley? No. I always moaned while eating it. Plenty of greens, no 'al dente' cooking then, the veg was boiled to death! We were made to eat our greens, which of course I hated, but what I did like was the water the cabbage was boiled in, it was delicious poured into a cup with plenty of salt and pepper.

The peas would arrive in pods and shelling them was a good job, it was almost impossible not to eat them while you were shelling them. The shout would go up "stop eating the peas and leave some for your dad's supper!" The peas were small, sweet and irresistible. There were enough peas to fill a colander but when we had finished shelling them, we were lucky if there were two thirds left. Potatoes, we lived on those, always boiled, thank god for the good old spud, they also served us well.

So did fish and chips. There were always plenty of chip shops around, three pence for a bag of chips, four pence for a large bag. Sometimes we would take old newspapers to the shop in exchange for a bag of chips. There was always a queue at suppertime, or teatime as we called it, it was as if the whole of Small Heath was in the chippy. Several decades later they had almost disappeared. Now it's trendy to eat fish and chips and even gastro pubs serve them. It has moved on from being the poor man's supper.

When summer arrived mom would keep the butter in a basin of water to prevent it from melting or going off. There was also a basin full of vinegar with diced cucumber and sliced onions packed into it. It was delicious. She would make jelly and blancmange and we would store them in the cellar and wait for them to set, it was cooler down there. Sometimes it would take days before they were edible. How much longer did we have to wait? "Be patient," we were told, "it's almost set."

We had lovely milky rice puddings, they were something else. Today you are able to buy rice puddings in tins, they are nice but not quite the same. Nothing compared to the way mom used to make it. When things became a little tight we would have semolina, it was all right but not quite the same. Tapioca that was something completely different, it was like eating warm frogspawn, but we ate it nevertheless. Maybe we were spoilt, on entering the house the smells emanating from the kitchen were a joy. Mom would be baking a cake or making apple pie, or jam roly-poly, treacle pudding and spotted dick. Yes, we were spoiled.

When my father was born in the Edwardian period, we were the richest and most powerful nation in the world but what happened to all that money? Whose pockets did it end up in? Certainly not the working man's. After the war you made sure you paid your rent, if not there was always a place waiting for you in the workhouse. We must not forget Ration Books either. How could you survive without them? Sometime in the latter part of 1953 sugar came off rationing, so people could go into a shop and buy a bag of sugar without a ration coupon, what a luxury, providing they could afford it. What we did have free was created by a wonderful welsh man. The NHS, what would our parents have done without it? We were the envy of the world, nobody else had anything like it, you might say it was a lifesaver. People moan and gripe about it today and they may have good reason to I don't know, but back then as far as I know nobody moaned. I think the working class deserved it. They certainly earned it.

Glitterball

When we lads reached manhood we started dressing up, slapping on Old Spice aftershave and headed off to the dance hall. Girls had become the most important thing in our lives along with The Tower Ballroom, the Casino, the Locarno and many more dancing establishments. The one thing they all had in common was the glitterball, dangling, spinning and revolving above the middle of the dance floor.

Many, many years later I was on a football tour in Portugal. I was coming to the end of my amateur football career, although I played into my early fifties and a bit of five a side in my sixties until my knee gave out and my body was telling me to stop. I also had the privilege of being on another tour of Portugal in my early thirties. The village we were visiting was rather remote and off the beaten track, no tourists, swimming pools or beaches. The people in the village were warm and friendly and my friend of many years, John who could speak a little Portuguese, was chatting to an elderly gent who was talking about his museum. He said he would like to show us his collection. John said of course we would love to see it, so John, myself and another friend trotted off with him to his museum, which was housed in small tall room in an odd looking building. Well the collection he had acquired, if you could call it that, at least half of it wouldn't have made it into a junk shop. I remember seeing this stained, torn print of the Queen in a cheap broken frame, which was his pride and joy. We of course were very complimentary about them, not wishing to hurt his feelings after all he did collect them.

The strange thing was everything appeared to be British. How he had acquired them heaven only knows! There were no British tourists living there so it was all rather peculiar. I did spot something hanging from the ceiling, which was the centrepiece to his collection, the 'piece de resistance', it was a glitterball! He then started to engage John in animated conversation, at the same time he was pointing towards the ceiling. When John finally managed to work out and translate their conversation it turned out the glitterball came from England, it came out of a ballroom in Birmingham. To think I might have danced under it!

Chimney Sweep

Chimney sweeps provided an important service in those days and probably still do today. You would often see the chimney sweep on his bike with brushes and rods attached to his bicycle and empty sacks or full ones depending on whether he was going to a job or on his way back from one. Of course he would be covered in soot, from head to toe! In the winter every chimney would be belching out smoke, no such thing as smokeless fuel back then. It was of paramount importance to have your chimney swept regularly as having a fire constantly burning meant the soot would build up inside the chimney.

When it was time to have your chimney swept, you would move all your furniture against the walls allowing the sweep access. Then you would cover everything up with whatever you could lay your hands on newspaper, brown paper, old bed sheets, whatever you could find. The sweep would cover the grate with his sack, it had a hole in the centre enabling him to push his rods and brush through, then carefully add more rods as he forced the brush up the chimney, dragging the soot down until the brush finally popped out of the top of the chimney pot. The sack covering the grate, whose job it was to protect the room from soot, always failed because it had more holes than a leaky colander. The result would be the room would be covered in a fine layer of soot, however hard you tried it was always be the same!

On one occasion when we failed to sweep the chimney the inevitable happened, the chimney caught fire. I was still quite small and I was promptly evacuated from the house to stand over the road where a crowd had already gathered. As we all watched the fire swirling round the roof, the fire brigade arrived. They dashed up the stairs to our bedroom above the living room and promptly smashed a hole in the chimney breast, which allowed them to hose water onto the fire, which swiftly put it out. They certainly knew what they were doing, it was all over almost as quickly as it started. The only down side was the living room floor was covered in dirty sooty water. But that was not a problem to mom, the most important thing she said, was that the fire was out and the house was still standing. But nevertheless it gave us all a fright.

Fog

I was able to find work in a carpenter's shop in Longbridge, thanks to my brother-in-law Frank, just round the corner from the Austin motor works, later to be known as British Leyland. It would be my last job working as a carpenter in Birmingham before I started work down the coalmines.

The carpenter's shop was more like a saw mill. We spent a great deal of time pushing long lengths of timber through a huge circular saw. There were no guards or proper protection, goggles what were they? Somebody would be at the front guiding the timber through the blade and somebody would be at the back supporting it and gently pushing it towards the saw. When the plank of wood was about three quarters of the way through the section of timber it would start to bend, slowing the blade down. The man at the front would leave his post and move to the front of the saw, then he would hammer a wedge between the two pieces of sawn timber allowing the blade to run freely, at the same time supporting the timber. The man at the back would take over the duties of guiding the final piece of uncut wood through the saw.

When the saw blade became too hot we would douse it with oil to cool it down. We became lazy about the cooling down procedure, you were supposed to brush the oil on when the saw was switched off, but most times we did it when the saw was still in motion. Crazy I know. How we avoided having a serious accident heaven only knows. Today it would be illegal, back then nobody cared. Years later when I was using a small circular saw with guards, protecting every possible angle and wearing goggles, I was a still a little apprehensive and I might add a tad nervous.

In the mornings I would have my obligatory drink of water, grab my sandwiches, skip down the back entry and jump on the number 58 bus into the city. I would then change buses and board the one heading down the Bristol Road to Longbridge. I always took my seat upstairs with all the smokers, the whole of the top deck would be full of smoke. Most people would be reading Andy Capp in *The Daily Mirror*, the only thing you could hear, apart from the rustling of newspapers, was the continual coughing and the clearing of the throats by the workers from the motor works. The only real downside of working out there was that we left work at the same time as the car workers so it would always be a scramble and queue for the bus back into the city. The atmosphere on the bus on the way home was completely different to the one coming. The workers were much more animated and listening to their conversations, almost made me feel as though I was working on the assembly line myself.

One dark, dank, cold evening in the middle of winter I walked all the way from Longbridge to the centre of Birmingham. I say walked, it was more like groped my way back to the centre of town. The reason being the fog had descended. It was nothing new it happened every year, I think they called them 'pea soupers'. But this particular evening turned out to be one of those, with a little extra spice, leaving me with little choice but to walk home. Visibility was zero, there was very little sound and everything appeared to be still. It had an eerie quality about it. I remember seeing this orange light in the distance, so I headed towards it, only to find it was a packed bus, crawling along at the same speed as me. So for safety reasons I decided my best option was to walk as far away from the kerb as possible. Luckily it was more or less a straight road all the way back to the city. On the odd occasion I would hear a horn pip or someone talking as they brushed past me, because everybody was in the same situation. I had the feeling I was on some kind of strange adventure, maybe in some kind of masochistic way I was enjoying it.

I don't remember how many hours it took me to reach town. I do remember the closer I got the easer it became, maybe due to a combination of the city lights and the fog lifting. By the time I had reached the other side of town and jumped on the number 58 bus heading home to the warm and comfort of No 13 Herbert Road, my adventure was already becoming a distant memory.

Nits

Cinderella, Hansel & Gretel, Babes in the Wood, these were wonderful fairy tales by the Brothers Grimm which my mother would tell me. She used them as bribery, she would tell them as she looked for nits in my hair, she was determined my hair would be a nit free zone when the nit nurse did her rounds at school to check. If you were found with them, you were sent home and it would have been too embarrassing. Everybody had them at some time or other, only they never owned up to, it was almost a crime.

Reluctantly I would sit in the chair as my mother dragged her fingernails through practically every hair on my head as she inspected me, she not only did it by sight but also by feel. She tugged on my hair, which drove me crazy, I hated it and would scream out "no more!" So to calm me down her ploy would be the Grimms' fairy tales, which of course I loved. Although I had heard them a hundred times before they never seemed to lose their magic. If she hit the jackpot she would then crack the nit between her thumbnails, you could actually hear it pop. It's funny my mother loved the sound - and so did I!

A Dish of Whelks

When I was still a small boy I accompanied my mother on her Saturday morning shopping trips to the Birmingham Bull Ring. She loved the market stalls and all the banter amongst the stallholders. They would all be calling out, making witty remarks, trying to sell their wares, it sounded as though they were trying to outdo each other in a friendly and jocular way. We would walk up and down the Bull Ring inspecting the stalls and then we would go up the steps into the market hall where there were even more stalls and more banter.

We always made our way to the corner that housed the fish and the stuff in shells. They were all laid out before us in neat rows: cockles, mussels and most important of all whelks.

My mother loved them, she introduced me to them and I have loved them ever since my very first taste, I still love them to this very day. You paid your money and you had your pick, you would then douse them with pepper and vinegar. My mother would check on me making sure I was ready to go, she would give me the nod, then we would tuck in. Most times my mother would have second helpings.

The love of whelks has never left me. If I am in a market, or by the seaside and there's a stall selling whelks then my taste buds will start tingling and off I go. Like mom I will sometimes have seconds. Today they are still laid out in the same way as they were all those years ago in the market hall in the Bull Ring in Birmingham, where I had my very first taste. The original market hall has long gone, even though it survived the bombing raids after being damaged during the war. It would survive, for many more years, but would finally succumb to progress. I suppose that's the way of the world.

A Pint of Mild

When it came to having a pint of mild there was no other city in the country that produced a better pint than the one produced in Brum, be it Ansells, Mitchell & Butlers or Davenports. They were, without question, the very best but you may think that's just a Brummie being biased. Alas you would be hard pressed to find one today, we have become a nation of bitter and lager drinkers. Me, I like a pint of real ale or a nice glass of wine, a malt whiskey or even a glass of champagne when I can get my hands on one!

The drinking culture today has changed since my days of necking pints of mild when I was growing up in the back streets of Birmingham. Maybe our palates have become more discerning. Back then a pint of mild was the order of the day. When I later moved to London, it was difficult to find a decent pint of mild, so I became a 'bitter' man and still am to this very day.

The mild if you could find it anywhere else in the country back then, looked and tasted like black unsweetened treacle so no wonder it disappeared. When the Blues, Villa and Baggies supporters went to London to watch their teams play the first thing they would say on entering a pub would be "a pint of mild please". Their reaction would be "what no mild?" or if they did manage to lay their hands on one the expression on their faces would be one of disgust.

In those days you drank the beer that your town produced. If you wanted to have a pint of Flowers you had to go to Stratford upon Avon. Of course everything is different today, we have kegs so it travels. You could be in a pub in Devon and have a pint brewed in Suffolk and now there are microbreweries popping up everywhere, it can only be a good thing if you like a nice pint of real ale. Cheers!

Rhododendron

In the summer months we would head for Elmdon, all the way up the Coventry Road to the bus terminal, just a couple of miles before you arrived at Birmingham airport. I believe it's all built on now, maybe back then it was part of the green belt. My earliest memory of going there was with my big sister Peggy, there were miles of fields some cultivated and some just left in their natural state and a stream which meandered through it. We would try to catch tiddlers with our hands.

As my sister grew up other things in her life became more important than chasing tiddlers in a stream but I continued going there with my friends and my brothers. The fields were there for everyone to see, they certainly weren't a secret but apart from my brothers and a couple of friends, I cannot remember anyone from Herbert Road or the surrounding areas ever going there. It was as if it was a secret garden that only we knew about. I think I must have been going there from the late forties to the mid-fifties then like my big sister other things in my life came to the fore.

On one occasion we wandered a little further than we normally would, when we came upon this beautiful pond covered in lily pads and water reeds, it looked a little too deep to wander into, so we kept to the perimeters. There were also bushes and bushes of rhododendrons in full bloom. My friend suggested we take some home for our parents, which I though was a good idea. So we proceeded to gather bunches and bunches of the huge flowers. As we clambered onto the bus home with our flowers and made our way upstairs, the bus was completely empty because there was always an empty bus waiting at the terminus. Sometimes you would sit and wait for half an hour or more, before you departed so as we sat there getting bored and impatient, we decided to place our flowers in the metal bar, which ran horizontally across the windows. We were sitting up front, so we covered the whole front window in flowers, wedging the stalks behind the metal bars.

We had so many flowers we ended up covering the whole of the top deck in them. Then we finally headed off towards home. As we approached various bus stops, we could see people looking up, they must have been thinking what kind of bus is this? I think it was one of those days when the shoppers decided to sit upstairs rather than downstairs. We just sat up at the front of the bus pretending we knew nothing about it, occasionally sneaking a peek behind us. We did notice the flowers were slowly disappearing, much to our amusement and when we finally reached our destination, our flowers were reduced to barely a bunch each. It could not have worked out better, when I entered the back door and greeted my mother with a bunch of flowers, she looked at me and said, "Sorry son I don't like them, it's bad luck to have wild rhododendrons in the house."

Another Accident

Our dad had spent most of his working life as a cobbler. It was a good honest trade. He was actually trained to be a shoemaker, but for most of his life he would just repair shoes, working in various shops around Birmingham. Towards the end of his working life he ceased being a cobbler and secured a job working at Lucas the motor parts company. He worked the night shift, which as far as I know he enjoyed. It was a change for him, a different environment and it kept him out of the pub. By then the dynamics of the house had changed. I had left home and David and Tony had already married. It must have quite peaceful at number 13, Dad out at work all night, so mom was left with just the two girls. It would have been as if a calm had settled over the place, although David was only working a few doors away at Bradleys the butchers and he popped in every chance he got. It would be the same with Tony. It was more difficult for me, but every chance I had I would go home at weekends.

The place was like magnet and it kept drawing us back. Although we argued and fought, we were a close family, I suppose we had so much history with each other. People are much more tactile with each other today, even strangers hug when they greet each other and kiss when they meet, I think it's a good thing. We brothers use to hold hands which some people commented on, otherwise I would never have been aware of it. Sometimes we would be sitting in the pub holding hands, maybe we were ahead of our time. Mom often said "If any of you had an accident, or became ill or were in any sort of trouble, we would all come running." We still do to this day.

One evening when mom and Sheila were sitting at home and dad had already left for work, there was a knock on the door. On opening it mom was greeted by a policeman, who then asked if he could come in as he had some distressing news to deliver. It seemed that on his way to work, some drunken lads in possession of a car had knocked dad over on a zebra crossing. It was a terrible accident, which turned out to be life threatening. The policeman very kindly drove Sheila and mom to the hospital where they found dad unconscious and about to have an emergency brain operation. The doctor informed my mother that his chances of survival were only 50/50. In those days you were not allowed to hang around the hospital, today she would be allowed to stay until the operation was over, but then she was presented with a plastic bag containing his clothes and his cap, covered in blood. She was then asked to leave and given a time when she should phone up and she would be given the results. Both she and Sheila then caught the bus home.

On New Year's Eve after several days in a coma, dad was given the last rights. It was the last day of 1963, the same year I moved out of Birmingham. How long he was in a coma for I don't really know. He made an amazing recovery, although still badly damaged, after several months he came home. He was not the same man as the one that went in. He only had one leg on entering the hospital and two when he was discharged, of course one was a tin one, state of the art for those days. He looked different, standing there with two legs and a walking stick, instead of one leg and two crutches. He was never able to work again. He was definitely a changed man. He couldn't remember anything about the accident, he only knew what he was told. He had slowed down considerably and he became much calmer, the anger and bitterness seemed to have drained out of him. He was always witty when he wasn't being nasty, but now you could joke with him and send him up, he didn't seem to mind. Maybe he realised he was lucky to be alive.

Dad never grew up in a loving family environment, he never knew his mother and father as we did. For all our hardships and poverty of sorts, we were loved and loved each other and still do to this day. He was institutionalised at a very early age, it was something he never talked about, maybe it was too painful for him. I am sure when he was in the home they did a good job taking in a 'cripple' and teaching him a trade. In those days having a trade was of paramount importance, not everybody was so lucky. But the home that had taken on the responsibility of caring for him had to stay within their parameters, so healing his emotional scars was his own responsibility. He was lucky in many ways to have all of us to care for him, we wanted the best for him. Nobody as far as I know bore him any ill will, especially David, who I have already mentioned, he looked after dad when mom died. Dad went to bed one evening and died peacefully in his sleep, perhaps he did all his suffering during his lifetime.

Moving On

After several years of waiting, but not really thinking about it or really believing it would ever happen, dad was finally compensated for his accident. He was given a lump sum of money, enough for my parents to purchase their own property. It would be a ground floor maisonette in the Sheldon area, they would be leaving Small Heath forever. They had carpets on all the floors, central heating, a bathroom and to cap it all an indoor toilet. Dad had his own bedroom and there was a proper kitchen with hot and cold running water, a small dining table and a window looking out onto their own little back garden. Carol was the only one left at home so she moved with them, like mom she had green fingers, so how did the garden look? Marvellous! Every time Carol has moved in her life, all of her gardens have looked marvellous.

Just after mom bought her new property and was still waiting to move in, the local council turned up and offered her a council house! She was next on the list and they were pleased to offer her new accommodation. Mom thought it was nice, but a bit late in the day, so she told them rather smugly "We don't need it now, we've bought our own. Thank you." I remember asking her how she felt when she was leaving Herbert Road for the last time. "I was sad. I had a little cry," she said, "after all I raised you all there. Wouldn't you be sad?"

Broom Behind the Door

When people said that years ago you never locked your doors at night, it was because you had nothing to steal! It's true we didn't have anything to steal but the reason we never locked our doors, however, was that we had lost the keys, not only to the front door but also the back door. We did have a bolt on the front door and that was put on when the last person came in at night, but not always knowing who the last person was the door was quite often left unlocked. The cry would often go up in the morning "Somebody forgot to put the bolt on the door last night!" The key to the back door had been lost long before the front door key, so the solution was to wedge the broom behind it. All a burglar would have had to do was give the door a shake and they would have been in. The only things of value we had, apart from ourselves, was the furniture, big bulky stuff and the logistics of removing it would have been difficult, plus the old man's snoring would have scared them off!

In the earlier days we did have a huge Bakelite radio, which worked off an accumulator and had to be recharged, then when we had electricity we had a radiogram. Money, we were always looking for it, but could never find any. Everybody was in the same sort of situation, so robbing your neighbour was never on our radar. On the odd occasion we lifted a piece of fruit from the fruit and veg shop, it was more of a dare than anything else, you would run past the shop and try to grab an apple or something. It was more fun than stealing. On one occasion when we were still quite small another kid and I went into a certain well-known store. When we came out he had a couple of golf balls in his pocket. Now what can you do with golf balls? You can't play football and you certainly couldn't play golf, at that time I never knew anybody who played golf. So that became the next dare, lifting golf balls until somebody was caught and given a good clip around the ear.

Gas Masks

Gas masks. Yes, we had them, but we never used them. After the mustard gas attacks in the First World War the various governments agreed to the banning of chemical warfare but of course they could not afford to take any chances, could we trust the enemy? No. So extra precautions were taken and gas masks were issued at the start of the Second World War. Every household and every person was presented with one. We kept ours in the cellar and we played with them occasionally. Nobody knew how to use them, well us kids certainly didn't and they just stood on the shelf in the cellar. I think they may have still been there when the family finally moved out many years later. It's difficult to comprehend that I lived through those dark days, those days of uncertainty. Imagine somebody knocking on your door today and issuing you with gas masks for you and your kids?

Part-time Job

When we became teenagers, some of the lads would find themselves employment doing a part-time job. I had a newspaper round and one summer holiday I had a job on a bread delivery round. We had our milk delivered, most people did, but having our bread delivered would have been a luxury. You never saw many, if any, bread vans down our road or the ones nearby. It was more the leafy areas of Brum, the nicer houses with front and back gardens, that was where you would find the bread vans.

There was a baker in Yardley and you could wait at the end of the drive for him in his van to leave and start his round first thing in the morning, you could then step forward and ask him if he needed help. To my surprise almost the first time I asked he said yes "Jump in". The first thing that struck me was the heat and smell of the bread gently wafting through the air. When you touched the bread you had to be careful how you handled it, if you were heavy handed it would easily lose its shape, you had to wait for it to cool down. The driver would pay you out of his own pocket. The guy that I was with was a bit on the mean side and I noticed if somebody off the street wanted to buy a loaf off him, he always charged them extra and I was also a little disappointed with my wages. By about the third week I was delivering most of the bread, he just sat in his van pretending to be doing his books and moaning at the same time, expecting me to memorise it all, but I still enjoyed doing it.

One very hot day he bought me a bottle of pop from a shop, I can still remember what it was called, it was my favourite - ice cream soda. I almost drank it in one go. By chance I drove past the shop a couple of years ago with my brother and it was still there. Different shop of course, but still a shop.

The house that still sticks out in my mind was the one with the bees. I would deliver the bread round the back of the building to the kitchen door which was always open and there were beautiful sponge type cakes everywhere. The lady that lived there seemed to be continually cooking. The first time I delivered I had a bit of a shock, there were hundreds if not thousands of bees, all around the doorframe. They were on the doorstep and they were piled up all over the window, all going about their business and I had never seen anything like it in my life, not then or since. I would just lean through the open door and hand her the loaf. I don't think the bees even noticed me. I found it fascinating and I enjoyed going there. Looking back it was an enjoyable summer.

Penicillin

I have already mentioned Lucas the motor parts company and makers of batteries, light reflectors and various other components. Everybody in Birmingham knew someone, or had a family member who worked there. I myself had two stints of being employed by them. They were a good company to work for if you liked that sort of work, but I didn't, my mind was somewhere else. I was entering those dark days I have already talked about, where I would be in and out of work, with the emphasis being on more out than in and would last until I left Birmingham. When I look back on my life, apart from losing loved ones, it was my unhappiest time ever, something that has been locked away in my mind.

My first job at Lucas was in the plastic moulding factory, which housed dozens of moulding machines. You would stand by your machine and feed it with the necessary material which would then be turned into a mould. You would close the gate, press the button, then the machine would slam shut. You would wait a few moments for the mould to set and you would then press the button again and the machine would then separate and you would open the gate, remove the newly pressed mould and place it in a box. Then start the procedure all over again, which would continue for the next eight hours. It was called 'piece work', the incentive being the more pieces you made the more you were paid. So if you were driven by money, which was of course the reason you were working there, then you never left your machine. Organic materials were slowly being pushed to the side, the world was turning to plastic.

I worked hard, the money was good and the foreman liked me. He asked if I was interested in moving forward, he said plastic was the future. I just said I was and I would do my best. He then told me I had the right attitude and I would do well. I just told him what I thought he wanted to hear, but it was not for me. I was working three shifts: the first week would be from six in the morning until two in the afternoon, then from two until ten o'clock at night, then from ten until six in the morning. Imagine what that did to your body clock? I was told your body would get used to it over a period of time. I was eighteen years of age and my wages were burning a hole in my pocket, I wanted to be out spending it. I didn't mind the six till two shift, it was the afternoon and night shift that were the killers.

How long I could have kept on working there for I had no idea. The decision was taken out of my hands. I felt this pain in my right leg just below the knee and every time I touched it I would jump with pain. Over the weeks it grew progressively worse. Eventually I was hardly able to walk, I just lay on the couch, I couldn't even climb the stairs to bed. The strange thing was my leg looked normal, it was the look on my face that set the alarm bells ringing, even though I had been visited by a doctor who said there was nothing to be unduly concerned about and suggested a poultice would be the solution. The following day, after a sleepless night, I was taken to hospital in an ambulance, the same one I visited years earlier with my broken leg, the now famous Queen Elizabeth Hospital. I went into hospital in the evening and was operated on the next day.

The diagnosis was I had osteomyelitis, a sort of bone infection with an abscess growing in my bone. I remember waking up after the operation and seeing the doctor who had operated on me, he was standing over the bed surrounded by what I assumed were medical students. It was bit like the film *Carry on Doctor*, he was firing questions at them as I lay there with my leg exposed and a tube sticking out of it, I was deeply embarrassed. With all those faces looking at me all I could do was grunt and grow redder in the face, I must have looked like a belisha beacon.

I would find myself in the same situation, fifty years later almost to the day in St. Mary's Hospital in Paddington, London. This time I wasn't the least embarrassed. I suppose I had become more mature and surer of myself. I had read many books since those early days, I had travelled, I had met and befriended lots of interesting people, I had performed on stage and I had made speeches and thought nothing of it. I have a bit of a reputation for telling jokes, some people have even claimed to have laughed. So this time when the professor asked me, at the same time he was examining me and talking to the students "Do you mind?" Of course I didn't mind. I had an audience, I was happy. We all chatted and I made light of my situation, much to the surprise and amusement, of the medical students. You're probably wondering how did I know it was fifty years since my last stay in hospital? Well it was the fiftieth anniversary of the Munich air disaster, when most of the Manchester United footballers perished on a snow covered runway in Germany in 1958. They were called the Busby Babes, named after their manager Matt Busby. I saw the Busby Babes play at St. Andrews, I saw them play Birmingham at Old Trafford and also play The Blues in the semi-final of the FA Cup at Hillsborough. All those great players and of course the great Duncan Edwards, who Bobby Charlton referred to as the greatest he ever played with. As you see football has followed me everywhere.

There was an older lad in the next bed to me, who had had a very bad motorbike accident. He told me it happened over the Christmas period and after being in a coma for several days, when he came round he thought he was in heaven. The whole ward was lit up with candles and there were people dressed up as angels singing carols. When he finally came to his senses he realised that he hadn't quite reached heaven yet and it was Christmas Day! Those weeks I stayed in hospital, I enjoyed. I had a good rapport with the nurses, I think they liked me and gave me a good send off when I finally left.

What I didn't like were the injections of penicillin every six hours, for more than two weeks. They used a long thick needle, with a long fat tube attached to it, the tube was full of thick, white, cloudy penicillin and it was administered at six in the morning, midday, six in the evening and midnight, every day for two weeks. At first I did not mind, I wasn't squeamish about needles, I never have been. It was the bruising it left on both sides of my thighs and my back side, they were the colours of the rainbow and they were very, very tender. I could hardly touch them. I used to watch the penicillin slowly being squeezed into me, who was I to complain, that white stuff they were pumping into me was doing its job. I read later the great songwriter Cole Porter, suffered from the same complaint and he being much older than me when he first contracted it would not have had the benefit of penicillin. I believe he suffered a lot and may even have lost his leg. Luckily I didn't lose my leg like my dad, we could not afford to have two invalids in the family. But I do have a scar I am quite proud of and St. Mary's Hospital in Paddington is where Alexander Fleming is credited with the discovery of penicillin.

Go-Carts

I remember the older boys making them. Their construction consisted of a long piece of wood and the wheels of an old pram, two at the front and two at the back. If you were lucky you had an axel at the front, enabling you to steer with a piece of rope or string tied to it. You would probably find the material to build them on a bombsite or in somebody's rubbish. Sometimes the wheels would be a little wonky or bent, making the go-cart a bit rickety and never seeming to run smoothly. Still we enjoyed it, scooting down the street falling off them, bashing our knees up. I don't think there was one kid in the street that didn't have cut knees. The go-carts never lasted very long, they were always falling apart, mostly when we were on them.

Another form of amusement were old car tyres, you would run alongside them hitting them with your hands to keep the momentum going. Herbert Road had a slight slope so most times when you reached the steeper parts you would lose control and it would fly away from you. You would keep your fingers crossed it would either fall over or steer off course and crash into the kerb. There was one time when a bigger boy was racing a tyre that was so big it must have come off a lorry. We were all sitting on the kerb watching when he lost control of it, the thing took off and headed towards the main Coventry Road much to our horror. As it picked up speed reaching the end of Herbert Road, with us kids in hot pursuit, we prayed it would go straight across the main Coventry Road and stop when it hit the kerb on the opposite side. But no! We watched with our hearts in our mouths as it made a beautiful left turn onto the main road. When we all reached the main road we saw the tyre careering down the middle of it at a rapid speed, as we watched it vanish over the top of the dreaded Kingston Hill, never to be seen again. So what did we kids do? We ran even faster in the opposite direction!

Marbles Followed by Conkers

Marbles was a game we all loved playing, it was very popular. Every kid would be walking around with marbles in his pockets, weighing him down. They were rather beautiful things, in magnificent colours like the rainbow. I never tired of looking at them. I am unable to recall buying my first marble, I don't think I ever did. The game we all played amongst friends and schoolmates was to roll a marble about ten or twelve feet away. The next boy would try to hit your marble with his, if he succeeded that marble would then belong to him. If he missed, he would leave his marble there, giving you the chance to hit his, if you did then that marble was yours.

Sometimes you could win as many as six at a time if you were lucky. I practised a lot and became very proficient. My pockets were soon bulging with marbles, much to my delight. I was forever counting them, something I never got tired of. When I joined the senior school, marbles disappeared out of my life, marbles were for juniors, not seniors. It was time to play conkers! When the magnificent horse chestnut tree shed its conkers that would be our time to start playing. Sometimes we would climb the trees, other times we would throw a stick hoping to knock them down, mostly on our heads. You have to remember we lived in a built up area. Conkers weren't exactly in abundance, they were usually a bus ride away. When you did get your hands on them, the practice would be to bore a hole through the centre, then feed a piece of string with a knot on the end. You would then be ready to smash each other's conkers to bits. The idea was that your opponent would hold his conker out and you would swing at it with yours, if you missed it would then be your opponent's turn. If you twitched, he would most probably miss and smash your knuckles instead, which would cause you to twitch in the first place. There was talk about banning it.

Toffee Apples

Mrs Miles was a little crumpled old lady, well that's how she appeared to us kids. In reality she was neither of those things. She owned the green grocer's and general provisions shop in Cattel Road opposite the Greenway Pub. In the summer time she kept her bacon in tomato boxes to keep it fresh and it appeared to work. Mrs Miles was famous in that part of Small Heath, not for keeping her bacon cool in the summer, but for her toffee and her toffee apples. In those days we would only eat things that were in season, but we always had something to look forward to. If I recall correctly, it would be the weekends when she sold her special treats and people would pop in on the way to the pictures and treat themselves. If something upset her she would refuse to make them, much to the disappointment of everybody.

I have eaten toffee apples in lots of different places, but nothing that could possibly compare to Mrs Miles's. Even the colour was different to everyone else's. My mother worked in the shop on the odd occasion, Mrs Miles liked my mother and my mother certainly liked her. Mom told us she once asked for her toffee recipe and various other goodies she created. Mrs Miles replied by saying, "Sorry Beat. No." (My mother's name was Beatrice but people called her Beat) She told my mother people were always asking for it, even well-known sweet companies had offered to buy it from her. She would say "The answer is and always will be the same. No. I will take it with me to my grave." Is it still out there? Who knows? Did she take it with her to her grave? Mrs Miles's shop and all the other shops along that stretch of Cattel Road have long since gone. They have all been gobbled up by the car park that is part of Birmingham City Football Club. I have roughly calculated that the Blues Chairman parks his car at the bottom of what was once Mrs Miles back garden.

Pots and Pans

Kettles and saucepans, what did we do with them when they ceased to function properly? When holes appeared in them and water started to seep out, did we throw them away? No. Today you would, but back then we very rarely threw anything away. You couldn't afford to. If you could repair it you kept it and repair it we did. You went to your local ironmongers and bought a packet of washers, little metal things that covered the holes making them watertight. How many washers were in those pots and pans? I dread to think. The kettle and big saucepan were amongst the most important items in the house, they were our source of hot water and we couldn't have done without them. We heated them up on the gas stove and the fire, we used them to fill the bathtub, which hung on the wall outside and we boiled our clothes in the pans. There was always a smell of carbolic soap emanating from the scullery. They were always on the go. As important as they were, they would always be the last things to replace. Funny that. Maybe it's because we could always repair them.

Lighting a Candle

On my first visit to Paris, I found myself in the beautiful church of Notre Dame. I didn't have a wish list of all the tourist attractions I wanted to visit, I just happened to find myself there. Maybe it was because I remembered seeing *The Hunchback of Notre Dame* with Charles Lawton, then later Anthony Quinn playing Quasimodo. To walk into this magnificent church that has stood there for hundreds of years, with its splendour and grandeur, it is the same church where Napoleon crowned himself Emperor of France, the sheer vastness of the inside is overwhelming. With its high vaulted central nave and beautiful, stunning rose windows, you can imagine Quasimodo swinging around the flying buttresses and clambering over the cathedral's legendary gargoyles on the way to ringing the bells when things weren't going his way. I did inquire about the films and I was abruptly told they were made there, or at least parts of them were filmed there. There I was in this beautiful church, asking the guide about films, when I should have been inquiring about the gothic architecture and the skill and craftsmanship that went into building this church, but after all I was only a naïve, wet behind the ears Brummie!

Several years later, I visited the church again. This time my purpose was to repeat something I did on my first visit and that was to light a candle for my mother. Like her I was never really a church goer but I know she would have loved the gesture and the fact that I was thinking about her, sadly I forgot to tell her about the candle. After my second visit, I promised myself I would remember. If I had been someone who attended church, maybe it would easier to remember, I never did and like the first time I forgot. She never knew.

Years later when she was dying from breast cancer, the family would take turns looking after her, she was then living in a council flat in Chelmsley Wood with dad and Carol. I would visit every weekend. On the train journey there I would go over in my mind all the questions I wanted to ask her but when I arrived, I couldn't bring myself to ask her. I assumed I knew everything about her, unlike dad she always talked openly about her life. When you are young, you think the world revolves around you and although I was approaching forty, I was still immature. I knew my mother was dying and of course I knew that no one is immortal, but I never quite believed it until it happened. My sisters and brothers were there to comfort her when her time finally came. She was 69 years of age. Somehow through her determination, courage, strength and her will to do things right, she was able to keep her dignity right up until the very end.

A few years ago I was in New York and by pure chance I found myself outside St. Patricks Church in Manhattan. I was just wandering around the place, doing a little sightseeing I had no intention of going there, but suddenly there it was right in front of me, the oldest Catholic Cathedral in the United States. This beautiful building wedged in between all those skyscrapers, I had read about it and I had seen it in those wonderful Hollywood films. I knew I had to go in and see it for myself. On entering I was greeted by what I can only describe as an explosion of candlelight. They were everywhere and just like Notre Dame all those years ago, I lit a candle. This time it was for my mother, my father and my brother David. Today if I find myself in a church, I light candles for all my family.

Television

One day television came to Brum, in the form of the new TV shop on the Coventry Road, next door to the Regents Pub. The Regents Pub was one of dad's watering holes, situated on the corner of Coventry Road and Herbert Road. If you crossed over Herbert Road, you would come to the bus garage, then after that was Kingston Hill. On the opposite side of the road was Kingston Terrace, or what was left of it after the bombing. By now most of the rubble had been cleared away and it was just wasteland, with a couple of dozen houses left standing and still occupied in the shadow of St. Andrews Football Ground.

One evening sometime in the early fifties most of the kids from the surrounding areas and a few grown-ups were all jostling for position in front of the TV shop window. Although the shop window was full of TV sets and had been for many months, today would be the day when one of those television sets would be switched on and begin transmitting. We had all seen films before, but never in a shop window and what's more the picture we were watching was my favourite film genre, that good old horse opera, The Western. General Custer was making his last stand against Crazy Horse and the Sioux nation. What a film, what an evening and what's more it was free!

By the time the film was over it was dark. Everybody lingered around the shop for a while after in good spirits and it is a day that is still clear in my mind. It would be a few years before one of those TV sets reached our house. When it did finally arrive, it would not be one of those fancy new ones, it would be a second hand one with a transformer attached to the top of it, which needed adjusting every time it went wrong. But transformer or no transformer, it was still a TV and it was ours.

Wow! We had our own television set. I was working, so I was able to put a deposit down and pay so much a week. There were lots of mates around who had television sets. Of course by now I was a young working man and the fifties were drawing to a close. With new friends from different streets and different areas, most of them, if not all, had televisions. So I knew what it was like to sit in somebody's house and watch it. To sit in your own house and watch it, now that was something special. It even impressed our dad, he started staying in during the evenings, much to our surprise. Everybody commented on it and I think we were all happy about it. I know mom was. Dad was embracing the new age of television. Today everybody has TV. If you happen to know someone who doesn't, then it is not because they can't afford it, it is because it's their choice.

Man in a Cannon

I wonder if kids today get as excited as we did when the circus comes to town? I suppose most kids would become animated when they are going somewhere so thrilling. Of course circuses are almost unrecognisable today, they have evolved because they had to if they wanted to survive and tastes have changed, kids are more sophisticated today, better educated and they mature much earlier than we did. We grew up playing in the streets and most kids, when they enquired about things, were told by their parents to stop asking stupid questions. How things have changed. More and more people are working from home, mothers take maternity leave and it enables them to spend more time with their children. Education begins at home. People understand more about other people's cultures or if they don't always understand it they are at least aware of it. If an incident happens in a remote part of the world, be it large or small, we don't even have to leave our beds and we can watch it unfold as it happens. The circuses today have to cater for a more sophisticated audience.

Maybe they have lost some of their magic like the lion tamer entering the ring with his whip in one hand and a chair in the other to keep the beast at bay.

When our circus came to town, it pitched its big top in a field in Hay Mills. Hay Mills was on the Coventry Road, about a mile behind The Holy Family School, it of course would be a special treat for us and an experience, somehow I always managed to get there. My most remarkable memory was of a man being fired out of the cannon. What the other kids went to see I don't know, but I was certainly there to see the Cannonball Man. It was the finale, this was what we were all waiting for. I had visions of him flying through the roof of the tent, never to be seen again and for once the lion tamer, the man with the performing fleas and the elephants, were all holding the show up, even the clowns ceased being funny. When at last they finally rolled out the cannon, it seemed like an eternity before the man appeared and climbed into it, waving to the crowds before sliding down inside the barrel. Now this was it, look out sky here he comes. But wait! There was the obligatory drum roll, which went on and on and on. I thought he might have fallen asleep, but how could he with all that noise? Then suddenly it stopped and a man appeared wearing something like coat tails, carrying a lit torch, as he stood over the fuse with the naked flame, the drums started up again. This was, to put it in modern day terms, the mother of all drum rolls. When at last he finally lit the fuse, we waited and waited, just when we thought nothing was going to happen and the act was something of a damp squib, there was this huge BANG, followed by a great bilge of smoke.

When we finally recovered our senses from the shock of the bang and the clearing of the smoke, we were all left seeing this man swinging in a net a few meters from the cannon. After the applause quickly died down and the lights came on, in less than a fraction of a drum roll, we were all hustled very quickly outside, leaving us to make our way home in the pouring rain. I don't think I have been to a circus since.

1963

The coldest winter I can ever recall was in 1963, although 1947 was reputed to have been as bad if not worse and I remember very little of it, if anything at all. When we were kids, the thing I most remember about winter, was my mother coming into the bedroom in the morning and opening the curtains, telling us there was snow all over the rooftops. We would all jump out of bed cheering. It was a wonderful sight. Although the snow stayed for weeks and weeks, we still loved it, even though we never stopped shivering. We seemed to have no concept of time, it's as if time stood still. Today when it snows, it rarely really settles. Back then there would be deep snow, then it would freeze, the temperature would rise slightly, then it would snow again and continue like that for weeks. It would all be banked up on the edge of the pavement and into the gutter, you would have to climb over it to cross the road and when it finally thawed, it would all turn into a dirty grey slush taking days to disappear.

The fountain behind the Town Hall in the centre of Birmingham was frozen over as we celebrated the arrival of the New Year, we were sliding on the ice when the chimes went up welcoming in 1963. After the last two or three years of despair and despondency and feeling like some sort of outcast, I had the feeling this would be my year. This would be the year my life would change forever. I kept telling myself it would and it did, although it would take several months before I would finally leave Birmingham.

I had this strong feeling my destiny lay somewhere else. I couldn't possibly go on living the way I was living, it wasn't fair on my family or myself. It wasn't Brum, it was me. Although I've ended up living most of my life outside of Birmingham, I still feel like a Brummie. When people say to me, "Oh, you're from the North," I say, "No, I'm from Birmingham, I'm a Brummie."

All the friends I have made over the years, even the ones I've lost touch with know me as a Brummie and they certainly know I am a Blues supporter. I am definitely not a Villa supporter but when they win trophies, which of course they do, I don't resent them I'm pleased for them, it's good for the city after all they are Brummies too!

Anything good that comes out of Brum is fine by me. I wonder how many train journeys and road trips I have made between London and Birmingham? In the early days I would hitchhike, I did that off and on for years. Something you never see now. It's like having a dual nationality: half Londoner, half Brummie. When I first went to London I never met any Brummies. Now we are everywhere, but maybe I am jumping ahead of myself.

Going back to the celebrations of 1963. Once it was over and we trundled our way back home in the freezing cold, I had a feeling of optimism. Something in the back of my mind was telling me 'If you wish hard enough for something, then it will happen'. Towards the end of the sixties and early seventies, I celebrated the New Year on several occasions in Trafalgar Square. I remember certain bits of it, but none of them are as clear as that freezing cold night we ushered in the year of 1963.

Friends

Had I become rich and famous, I would have mixed with other rich and famous people. Alas, I never became either rich or famous. I don't know if it was by chance, or by being in a certain place at a certain time, but I did manage to meet some famous and interesting people and make friends with them.

I found that when I met people who were well established and seemed worldlier and more sophisticated than myself, on the occasions that I found myself observing, listening and talking to them, I hoped it was possible that some of their sophistication and worldliness might brush off on me. Even more so when they showed an interest in me and responded in a positive way. I then realised that all the things that I believed and strived for, that I had hoped were out there, really were and it was possible for me to become part of it.

Slowly my life changed and once it did, I found it was impossible for me to go back. I didn't see it changing, it just happened. I think it's important that you must never forget or lose touch with where you came from and who you are. I was very lucky to meet such lovely people within a couple of years of leaving Birmingham. It seems much easier to me today to breakout of your environment, but back then it was a little harder. The class system, which still exists today, appears much more relaxed than back then. Most people today go to university and apart from education, it also gives you a chance to broaden your outlook, mixing with people of different backgrounds and different cultures. Yes, the world has certainly moved on.

More Friends

In 1968 I joined a park football team in London, which was formed a decade earlier by a bunch of Cambridge graduates. When I joined the team, most of them were in their mid to late thirties and some were on the verge of retirement. It was a Sunday league team, which suited me because Saturday was for watching football. I would go on to play for them for the next twenty-five years or more, well into my fifties. My very first game for them was a day trip into the country, after the game the host cracked open a barrel of beer on the side of the pitch and I thought, this is for me! I still have the photograph that was taken of the teams after the game.

I would begin friendships with some of those young men, which still endure to this day. Later on I would also play with five of their sons, who are also my friends. Most of the original team were involved in the literary world and journalism and would go on to establish themselves. Three of them would become Professors and one was knighted for his services to the Government. The rest were only brilliant! I am also still friends with the younger players that joined the team when I had become an older player.

When Easter came we would embark on our weekend football tours, a couple of times to Portugal, several times to France including Brittany and Normandy, twice to Dublin and a couple of times to Jersey, Germany and Holland. The Germany tour came near the end of my career, we called it the 'Father and Sons' tour and it would be my last. My abiding memory is crossing the ball for one of the team, Leo, to head home the winner. We also took many trips in England: Devon, Cornwall, Yorkshire, Wales and many other places, all paid for by ourselves. Because of certain connections in the team, when we travelled abroad, we were sometimes treated like kings, we had receptions laid on for us and the national anthem was played before the game. We were certainly looked after, although we lost more games than we won. Not bad for a park football team.

We also played against a couple of Oxford colleges and Brighton University. The team became a big part of my life and I also ran it for many years, some of the younger players look on me as though I am still their manager. We still get together, most times it's just an excuse to talk about old times. Sadly we have had a couple of funerals with the passing of the original members, which also gives us another chance to get together. We regale ourselves with stories of memorable games and funny incidents. We may have even created our own folklore. It's also flattering that some friends have mentioned me in books that they have published.

Stinging Wasps

One bright summer's day, when he was about seven years old, my brother Tony and a friend were playing in the fields at Elmdon when he was dared to jump across a stream to the bank on the other side. With a good run up he managed to achieve it, but with great shock, horror and complete surprise he landed on a wasps nest. Suddenly it all turned into a nightmare. He ran screaming towards the main road, with the wasps swarming all over him continually stinging him. Luckily, a lady who was walking past came to his rescue, calmed him down and helped chase the wasps away. By then Tony was in a terribly distressed state. The lady took him to a doctor's surgery nearby and when the doctor pulled off his shirt there were wasps still stinging him.

I wasn't there to witness it, but I was there when she arrived with him at the back door. She had very kindly brought him all the way home on the bus. I was shocked when I saw his face, it was completely misshapen. My mother arrived home from work shortly afterwards and was horrified at what she saw, she took him straight to the hospital. That evening when he came home, he was calm but still traumatised. Later that night, just before we were about to go to bed, I heard a noise outside the back door. Because the back entry led to the main Coventry Road, people would on occasion wander up when it was dark, some people never liked to use it at night, but it never bothered us kids. On hearing the noise I quickly ran to investigate. I opened the door and was surprised to see the lady who had brought him home, I invited her in but she declined saying she could see Tony through the curtains and she was relieved to see he was fine. She was worried about him and felt she had to come back and see for herself if he was alright. As she walked away, I couldn't help but think what he would have done without her help. It was obvious that she was a kind and very caring person.

Three-penny Bit

A three-penny bit was about the same size as a modern day pound coin. When my little brother David was playing around with one in his mouth he accidently swallowed it causing a degree of panic in our house. We had no idea then what damage it could cause, but it meant yet another trip to the hospital for mom. David had an x-ray and the coin was located, it was sitting in his stomach. The doctor told mom not to worry, it should work its way out. He suggested that

David's poo should be checked every time he went to the lavatory. Poor old gran was given the job of doing the checking, which of course she did diligently every day, with very little reward. She failed to find it. The three-penny bit was lost forever. Who said 'where there's muck there's brass?' If there was it certainly wasn't in our house.

Nylon Stockings

I first remember becoming aware of nylon stockings when my big sister and her friends started wearing them. At the time I couldn't understand what all the fuss was about. Later on things would be different, but that was in the future. It must have been difficult for the girls because stockings cost money and they weren't cheap. I remember them removing the new stockings from the packets they came in and making a ladder in them before they had chance to put them on. Just catching a thread of the nylon could cause a ladder and the tear would run all the way down the stocking thereby making them useless before they even had chance to wear them. They were called ladders, because that's exactly what they looked like, a ladder. Once the ladder started to run it was difficult to stop it. The solution was nail varnish, which seemed to be the magic formula. I used to feel sorry for the girls when it happened, all that money paid out would be gone in seconds. It wasn't 'proper' or lady like for young girls to go out with ladders in their stockings.

The girls loved stockings as they gave colour to pale, white legs. I suppose today the modern equivalent would be a spray tan. The stockings also made the girls feel glamorous and it was uplifting for them, after all they had lived through some dark and austere times. Then, of course, there was the seam at the back of the stocking. The dreaded seam! Keeping it straight at the back of the stocking was of paramount importance, girls were always asking you if their seams were straight. A few years on when I started to take an interest in girls legs and other parts of their anatomy, when a girl walked past somebody would say "Wow! I fancy her." Then some other wag would reply saying "Yes, but did you notice her seams weren't very straight?" You would all nod in agreement and suddenly she wasn't so fanciable.

During the war when the Yanks were here, they were laden down with them although we didn't see too many of them in Small Heath! When we did bump into them, I was told to ask if they had any 'gum chum', which the Yanks found very amusing, as they handed me a stick of gum. They were very generous. My sister would have been too young when they were dishing out the nylon stockings and it would be a few years yet before stockings became part of her life. They were held up with a suspender belt a few inches above the knee. On a rare occasion if a girl was wearing a shortish skirt, when she sat down the skirt would sometimes rise up, exposing her suspenders and maybe a little peek of the white flesh above her stockings. Well I can tell you that was a treat for us lads.

School Phobia

We all played truant at one time another, missing the odd day or two of school. When we were in infant and junior schools we never thought about it, but when we became seniors that would be the time we would start opting to skive off. Then the school board man would come calling. Yes, we would run for cover when we saw him on the horizon.

My brother David took it to another level, he just refused to go. I think it was in his final year, so they had no alternative, they had to put him in a special school, a sort of mixture of boarding school and borstal, a kind of boot camp. He was not a criminal, he just refused to go, I suppose that's a crime in itself. So for weeks that was his new home, where he would sleep, work, study and be disciplined. Unfortunately for mom the school was out in the country and difficult to get to without a car. It would mean catching several buses, then a very long walk down a country lane. A couple of times she did manage to get a lift in Frank's car, he was my sister Peggy's husband. On one occasion dad came, it was a long walk for him down the never-ending country lane, but he did it. When I visited David, he looked as if he was enjoying himself there, but still counting the days until he came home.

Walking back down the lane afterwards, I remember mom being upset. "Don't worry," we said, "he will soon be back home getting into trouble." We all laughed, but of course she still worried. When he came home, he started playing truant again and this time he was taken to see a Psychiatrist. He was diagnosed with having school phobia. He was just a few weeks away from leaving school altogether, so they decided he would complete his schooling at the special school and back he went! I don't think he liked the idea of leaving home but I think he preferred his new school to his old one, even though they had freezing cold showers first thing in the morning, something he enjoyed doing for the rest of his life. They were made to scrub the floors sometimes with a toothbrush. He told me when they had the school concert he sang a lesser-known Elvis song entitled 'I Want to Be Free'. I laughed when he told me there is a line in the song which goes 'I look out of my window and what do I see? I see a bird way

106

up in a tree. I want to be free, free, free as a bird in a tree.' He said on that line he walked over and looked out of the window. He had a great sense of humour.

David was physically very strong, very tough and slightly accident-prone. Whenever he injured himself he never made a fuss. Carol told me he once trod on a spike that went through his foot, he just jumped in his car and drove himself to the hospital. Mom said when we were little, we were always throwing stones at each other and they nearly always landed on David's head.

One morning years later when he was working for Tony, David failed to turn up for work, which was very unusual. Tony suspected something was wrong and he decided to go to his house. David's van was still parked outside, so he knew he was still in, even though his wife Sheila had already left for work. After calling to him through the letterbox, without getting a reply, Tony then decided to climb over the garden wall and break-in through the back door. He found him lying on the bedroom floor unconscious. David had suffered a brain hemorrhage and he never regained consciousness.

He was only forty-seven and it's hard to believe he has been gone for so many years.

David

Standing outside the church at David's funeral, watching all the people milling around and the cortege of cars which followed the hearse, it seemed to go on forever. I knew he was popular and I was pleased to see all those people, some of them were from way back, from the time he worked at Lucas.

At the time he passed away he was working with our brother Tony, who had a couple of carpet shops and a shop you might describe as a sort of bric-a-brac or second-hand shop. They started doing house clearances and they were becoming interested in antiques. The second-hand shop was changing every day, becoming more like an antique shop and they loved it. All the shops were next door to each other. David had a certain charm and rapport with the customers they liked him and he was popular. They were all there to say goodbye to him. Tony handled all the funeral arrangements, he organised it so the cortege would pass by the shops. It was, I thought, a nice touch and very moving.

They were both hard workers, six days a week and on many evenings they also did house clearances after the shop had closed. They grew up together and they were like The Bisto Kids, if you can remember them, but they never lived in each other's pockets, they had their own lives. They were completely different characters but they relied on each other. They were very quickly learning the value of the items they were collecting. After they did a house clearance, on arriving at the shop in the morning, there would be the dealers sitting in their big Volvos waiting for the shop to open, knowing they were dealing with a couple of guys who had no idea of the value of the antiques. But Tony and David were learning very quickly, they were picking the dealers' brains faster than they realised. They would stick a label on an item with a price tag of about ten pounds and another label next to it with SOLD on it. A dealer would look at it and say that's a ridiculous price I would have paid at least a hundred for it. When the dealer left they would take the labels off and put it in the storeroom. After a few weeks they would put it back in the shop with the price tag of one hundred pounds, they were catching on pretty quickly!

One time when I was there a dealer wandered in. David pointed to a new item they had just acquired and asked him how much he thought it was worth. "You're not picking my brains, David," he said. "I'm not," David replied, "I've just had a five pound bet with Tony that you could get within a tenner of what it's worth." The dealer suggested a price, David said "Tony you owe me a fiver, I told you he was good." When he left I asked David how he knew what it was worth. "I didn't" he said "we were picking his brains," as he handed Tony his fiver back. So off it went into the storeroom for a few weeks to appear later with a price tag on it, very kindly supplied by the dealer.

Of course when David died it was a terrible shock to us all. Tony put on a brave face, but I knew he was hurting. How he organised everything so brilliantly, was a miracle. I remember standing in that churchyard, thinking I would like to live to a ripe old age, but if I did would all my friends be around to say goodbye to me? It was very comforting to know he was well loved. It's hard to believe he has been gone all these years, I still see him clear and fresh in my mind. The smallest things remind me of him. If I see someone driving a car and his arm is dangling outside the window, I think of him, David always did that. He may be gone but he is not forgotten and he is still with me. Tony arranged for his ashes to be placed in the grave with mom and dad, he now rests with them.

New Music

It started for me about the same time I started work. There was this American guy called Bill Haley and his band The Comets, playing music that would change our lives, it was called rock and roll. Suddenly we were all rocking round the clock, sitting in the cinema watching the curtains open and all that music bursting out and the words 'One, two, three o'clock, four o'clock rock....'. The whole cinema, even the usherettes, would start shaking their bodies or tapping their feet. In some cinemas people got up and started dancing. A revolution had started, the rock and roll revolution.

Our parents weren't too happy, but we were. One man famously said he would climb up a tree and wouldn't come down until it was all over. If he's still up there, he is probably bald by now! The music only got better when Elvis Presley arrived, the Voice or the King as he was later called. Great rock and rollers like Chuck Berry, Little Richard, Jerry Lee Lewis and many, many more. It couldn't get any better. Black singers in America were segregated but when they came to Britain there were thousands of adoring white kids waiting for them. We loved them and I hoped they liked us. I read somewhere that they didn't like our food, no hamburgers, no hot dogs, no fried chicken, after all they were austere times we had only just shaken off the shackles of ration books. I can just picture all these great performers, whose records I collected, sitting in the back of a bus on a freezing cold dark night somewhere in Britain, with a newspaper full of fish and chips, heading towards a venue, where thousands of white kids were waiting for them. They must have been a little puzzled to say the least. It would be these performers that would help start our own musical revolution, a few years later, with The Beatles, The Rolling Stones.... Practically every city in the country was producing great bands, giving us a great musical heritage that we are still proud of today.

With the coming of rock and roll, came a new style of dress. Some reverted back to the Edwardian times and called themselves Teddy Boys. I never became one, they were a couple of years older than me, although I did copy the hairstyle, the D.A., short for ducks arse! It would mean combing your hair over at the back.

I never did really follow dress codes. Some years later when I was living in Brighton with my brother Tony, the Mods and Rockers turned up. Thousands of Mods and a handful of rockers, who were vastly outnumbered. The big fight on Brighton Beach, never really happened, I know because I was there. People were just running around, charging here and there. I said to my brother, if you find yourself amongst the Rockers, remember you're a Rocker. If you find yourself amongst the Mods, then you're a Mod. He always remembers me saying that. There may have been a few skirmishes here and there, but the real fighting started a few years later on the football terraces and we all know what happened there. But I digress. It's music I was talking about, not punch-ups.

The music we were listening to when we were growing up was borrowed from our parents it was great music, I still listen to it today, but this music was new and it belonged to us. It gave us a feeling of freedom. It allowed us to express ourselves. It was almost as if it was giving us a new sense of identity. Whatever it was we certainly embraced it. Today if you are at a party or a wedding, or some kind of celebration and they play a pop song, whether it be old or new everybody will join in singing the words. The radio would play a big part in it and of course later TV gave us our own rock and pop stations. As time went on they gave us more and more. Pop songs can be very evocative, most music can stimulate and arouse emotions in you. Today we can listen to the latest and the oldest all day long. It's a luxury we never had when we were growing up.

Sales Reps

A few years after I left Herbert Road, they started building a new estate. It would, at that time, be one of the biggest in Europe. The chosen name for it was Chelmsley Wood, a name now familiar to every Brummie. I believe at one time it was part of the Forest of Arden, as in Shakespeare's Forest of Arden, of course now long gone. There would be open green playing areas, houses with front and back gardens, indoor toilets, bathrooms and central heating. Things that people wouldn't normally have then. The concept at the time was good and I think the powers that be were trying to do the right thing. Some of the people from our neck of the woods would move there. My sister Shelia still lives there to this very day. She had all her children there, her grandchildren, even her great grandchildren.

It was about this time that the factories started disappearing. Certainly times were changing. More and more men were becoming salesmen and it was fashionable to refer to yourself as a 'Rep', short for representative, of whatever company you were working for. Some of them would not settle for the mere title of 'Rep' they would elevate themselves to a higher plane and call themselves 'Executive Reps'. I asked my brother Tony, who was a carpet salesman at the time, what an Executive Rep was he told me he was somebody who carried a briefcase and the contents of the briefcase would contain his banana sandwiches and a copy of *The Daily Mirror*!

A new breed of person was on the horizon and he was wearing a suit to work. Practically every Rep in Brum was now heading to the new Chelmsley Wood Estate and I am sure it was happening in other parts of the country with the construction of other new estates. People wanted new furniture, new curtains and certainly new carpets, in every room. It was pure luxury, almost decadent and why not? My brother Tony was a good salesman, he made a lot of money at this time for his employers so later on he would start to work for himself. He told me that all the floors throughout the flats and houses were made of a strong dark Bakelite material, called Marley Tile. He spent a good few years measuring miles and miles of Marley Tiles so his nickname for the estate was Marley Tile Alley.

At the time of him telling me these stories I decided to write a poem about it, with the help of my brother. I called it 'The Ballad of Marley Tile Alley'. It was, of course, about a carpet salesman and we upgraded his job title from 'Executive Rep' to 'Super Rep'. He was so good we even supplied him with a personal chauffeur.

The Ballad of Marley Tile Alley

The Super-Rep and his chauffeur,
The chauffeur's name was Don,
Said the Super-Rep to his chauffeur:
'Get the carpet samples and let's be gone.'

'For we are going to Marley Tile Alley,
Which is the Chelmsley Wood Estate,
To carpet the hall, stairs and the landings,
And the floors around the grate.'

Said Don to the Super-Rep:
'I think it can't be done,
Because the Chelmsley Wood Estate,
Has thousands of houses on.'

Said the Super-Rep to Don:
'That is not the right attitude,
Just watch me sell the carpets,
When I am in the mood.'

'I just walk into Hallways,
And throw the samples down,
Say choose your colours, dear,
While I measure all around.'

Said Don: 'I'd like to see it,
For this is my first day,
I've heard so much about you,
I hope I'm here to stay.'

The car was all packed up,
With samples of all kinds,
The colours in abundance,
Of different grades with wiggly lines.

The first door they knocked on,
The woman said: 'Come in
I think I'll have the champagne colour,
Or one with roses in.'

'Would it be a foam back madam,
or something more refined?
Say and Axminster or a Wilton,
Or something in that line?'

'An Axminster or a Wilton,
Of those I'd rather choose,
But unfortunately for me sir,
My husband tends to booze.'

'How often does he go out drinking madam?'
The Super-Rep did say,
At the same time he caught a glimpse of Don,
Who was looking in dismay.

'Every night it is Sir,
He spends no time at home,'
'Say no more,' the Super-Rep said,
'You'll have to have the foam.'

Said Don on their departure:
'I was sure that you were beat,
But when she saw the foam back,
That swept her off her feet.'

'Say no more,' the Super-Rep said,
'While I knock upon this door,
I'll make another sale here,
Of that you can be sure.'

The door it did fly open,
The woman she stood there,
Her fag was in her mouth
With hair curlers everywhere.

'I'm sorry to disappoint you fellows,
But I'm left without a bob,
I haven't worked for three months
And the old man's without a job.'

As Don stood there in great despair,
The Super-Rep did say:
'That's ok with me madam,
Just buy the underlay.'

'Well, there's nothing more I can say' said Don,
'After that excellent display,
Let's hope they get a job soon,
So they can cover the underlay.'

They both went on from door to door,
Selling carpets by the score,
The Super-Rep he seemed pleased,
Because the carpets sold with ease.

'I wonder how long it would take,' said Don,
'To carpet this whole estate?
I should think at the rate we're going
Somewhere around half eight.'

'You are right my boy, of that I'm sure
I think I'll knock upon this door,'
So that they did but no one came,
It seemed that they would wait in vain.

Then at last a voice cried out,
'Who's knocking on our door when my wife's out?
State your business and be gone,
It's time I got the decorating done.'

'I've been down grove and close and lane,
And sold all carpets of different names,
And street and road and avenue,
And whatever carpet will suit you.'

'Clear off again' the voice did say,
'We won't be buying any carpets today.'
'Well that's Ok,' the Super-Rep did say,
'We'll come back later anyway.'

'Well Don I think it's time we stopped and had a break,
You know I really fancy a large steak,'
Said Don, 'Of that I can't complain,
I trust I'll have one just the same.'

The Grapes it was where they went in,
The Super-Rep ordered a large Gin,
A pint for Don with no word said,
Because that man was in their head.

'Now that we have had our break,
And have polished off our steak,
I think it's time that we went back,
And sold that fella a foam-back.'

He knocked upon the door, the man came out
The Super-Rep said, 'Before you start to scream and shout,
At least give yourself a chance to hear me out.
I want to give you some advice
On how to make your house look nice.
If you are painting the walls and ceilings through,
Don't forget the floors they're important too.'

'I must admit' the man did say,
'I never really thought of it that way.'
'Well that's Ok' the Super-Rep did say.
'Don pass the tape so we can be on our way.'

The afternoon went flying by,
The carpet sales went high and high,
The evening came the Rep did say:
'I think we've done enough today,
Don if it's like this tomorrow too,
I shall be giving a bonus to you.'

Larindra

I don't remember the year, I don't even remember what age I was, but what I do remember is that I was one of the bigger boys when he arrived in Herbert Road. Suddenly he was there playing with all the smaller kids, he being the smallest of them all. 'He' was an Indian boy named Larindra and very quickly he became the most popular and the most befriended kid in the street. Everybody loved Larindra. He never stopped talking, he never stood still, he never walked up and down the street he ran up and down the street. If he wasn't running he was bouncing up and down the street. He was always cheerful and happy.

The only time he appeared calm would be when he was in the local shop with his mother, translating for her. At that time his parents couldn't speak English, but from the moment he arrived he was speaking perfect Brummie. I don't know where in India he came from, or how or why he got here, but he was here and he was one of us. One day I was standing on the front doorstep, watching all the kids running down the road at full pelt. All of them shouting with excitement as they headed towards the Kingston Cinema to watch the Saturday morning matinee and who was at the head leading the charge? None other than Larindra himself.

Some years later, when I was back home visiting my parents, I didn't know at the time that they would be soon leaving Herbert Road forever. By then my father had had his accident, so now he was at home. I was sitting in the living room and he was on the front doorstep talking to someone. I could hear him telling whoever he was talking to, that I was home for a few days. He invited him in to say hello to me. The heavy curtain that divided the two rooms was being pulled and tugged in all directions. I wondered what was going on. I was even more surprised when this turban appeared with this big brown hairy face under it, he then said in a Brummie accent, "All right Pete?" It was Larindra!

The last time I had seen him he was the smallest kid in the street, now he would have been the biggest. I suppose there's a lot to say for meat and two veg! He had left Herbert Road some years ago and he told me his family had moved up north. I told him I had no idea he was a Sikh, he told me his dad cut his hair and never wore a turban. I then recalled he had tied his hair in a bun on top of his head and when he let it down it would hang somewhere round his waist. In those early days I'd never even heard the word Sikh. We were sitting down facing each other, so he wasn't jumping up and down, or running round the room, but I could still feel that warm energy radiating from him, it was infectious. He told me he was in Birmingham on business and found himself wandering up Herbert Road. When he left, I stood on the front doorstep and waved goodbye to him. I'd like to think he had a happy childhood growing up in Small Heath, he certainly had plenty of friends.

A Short Encounter

Today when you pass someone in the street who may have some sort of deformity, disfigurement or is different in some way our general reaction is to look away out of embarrassment or politeness. The truth was nobody knew how to behave in those circumstances back when I was growing up.

When my sister Sheila was a little girl, we were walking down the road holding hands. We were going somewhere, quite where I cannot recall. When I mention it to my sister, she remembers the occasion very clearly, but she can't remember where we were going either! Anyway, we were ambling down the road without a care in the world, when suddenly as we were passing this entry, a man suddenly appeared almost bumping into us. He was a dwarf. The moment my sister saw him, she shouted out in a loud voice "Look at that little man!" I was horrified. He glared at us then kept on walking. I think he realised she was only young. She always remembers the ticking off I gave her. After I calmed down, I was able to see the funny side of it.

Today things are a little better I hope!

Uncle Joe

Mom's younger brother Joe was married with two children, our cousins Kenny and Margaret. Margaret was a few weeks older than me, she was born on the 3rd September 1939, the day the Second World War started, Uncle Joe said her birth was the reason that it started! He was always joking. We loved his jokes, he was always making us laugh. He would say to us "Go to the shop and ask them if they have any broken biscuits. If they say yes then tell them to mend them!"

He was a good brother to mom, she would go to him when she needed help. When he was called up in the war, he was sent to Malta. Mom and his wife Aunt Esther accompanied him to the train station to wave him off. Aunt Esther, was pregnant at the time with Kenny and it would be years before Uncle Joe returned home, his son Kenny would be four years of age before he laid eyes on him again.

I spent the first twenty years of my life growing up and playing with Margaret and Kenny even though they lived miles away. Uncle Joe loved and adored his children, it was as if he was making up for the missing years, they were a close family.

When Kenny reached the age that would enable him to drive they bought a car, a brand new one, a luxury in those days. They decided to take Gran on a day trip to the seaside as she had never seen the sea and giving Kenny some valuable driving time. Unfortunately they had a crash on the way there, nothing too serious but leaving them a little shaken up. It didn't seem to bother Gran, she just sat passively in the back of the car, waiting for it all to unfold. When it was all resolved, they found they had lost precious time so when they finally arrived at their destination, it was time to turn round and come home. Gran would now see the sea for the first time in her life, albeit only through the back window of a car! That would be the one and only time Gran ever went to the seaside.

A few years later Uncle Joe would be diagnosed with lung cancer. He was still in his early fifties and was still joking right up until the end. It was a big blow to Aunt Esther, Margaret and Kenny, he was their whole world. Mom lost a wonderful brother, Gran lost a wonderful son and we lost our Uncle Joe.

Cousins

There he was in our front room in his sailor's uniform, bending over his suitcase handing out goodies to my mom and dad. It was the first time I remember seeing him. He was my cousin Jimmy, he was home on leave and the first place he headed for was to see my mom and dad. I had no idea at the time that he was on leave from the Russian convoys. Churchill referred to them as the worst job to have in the war. Jimmy told me many years later, when he finally talked about it, that he did the trip about a dozen times and survived them all. He was there when they sank the *Scharnhorst*. His ship was the destroyer the *Onslaught*. He has now been awarded with medals from the Russians, even a visit to the Russian Embassy, but nothing from his own country, those that were on the Russian convoys are the almost forgotten heroes. If they are going to award him a medal they must move quickly, he is now in his nineties.

Now I am getting a little ahead of myself. Jimmy came home on leave a couple of times and he always arrived with goodies, then one day after the war he arrived at the back door with his new cockney wife Ann. He always called her Nancy and she was also in the navy. She was good to us kids and they were a perfect match. They settled in Birmingham and had five children, two boys and three girls. I grew up playing with the two elder boys, Alan and Paul. Jimmy never talked about the war till he was much older, but he loved regaling us with stories about his childhood, especially the time he was living in Bradford Street in Digbeth. His mother died when he was still a baby, so sadly he never knew her. He was brought up by his dad, who was also named Jimmy, and they lived in a back-to-back house with his brother Tom, Jimmy's uncle, who was my father. Uncle Tom was a single man at the time, he would later marry my mom and produce his own family, including me. Jimmy would tell us how his dad and his Uncle Tom were always fighting and he was stuck somewhere in-between. It would be his Uncle Tom who would look after him and it would be his Uncle Tom who made sure he was washed, dressed and ready for school. One day he was sent home because he had nits in his hair, so his Uncle Tom marched him back and berated the teacher. His Uncle Tom would also be the one he always gravitated to.

One of my favourite stories was the time he was given half a crown to go and pay the woman who looked after him during the school holidays, when his dad and Uncle Tom were at work. When he was walking past the pub in Bradford Street there was a group of men standing outside. He started teasing them, showing them the money and saying "look what I've got!" tossing the coin in the air in front of them until somebody stepped forward, cuffed him round the ear and snatched the money out of his hand, then disappeared into the pub to spend it. In tears and with no money Jimmy had to go back and face the music. With his ear still ringing after the slap, just wait until he arrived back home! He was always getting into trouble, but he would always laugh about it, he would tell stories with such enthusiasm it was compelling. His own kids knew them better than we did. It's rather refreshing to think his early childhood, growing up without his mother and then going into the navy on the convoys, wasn't exactly a walk in the park yet he is still able to talk about it as if it was.

A True Romance

One evening in 1975, I was visiting a friend's house with a couple of other friends, when this beautiful girl appeared with her young son. I opened the door for her, pretending I was the butler. Her young boy had come to spend the night with his friend, so off he ran to a different part of the house to play with him, leaving me to very quickly engage his mother in conversation!

I had just been working in rep in Manchester and I was back in London out of work, with no money. The money you were paid in repertory theatre was barely enough to live on. Chris, an actor friend of mine, had written a play and would be directing it at a lunch venue in Leicester Square. They were called fringe plays, there was no money involved, but that was the way in the fringe theatre. You did it for the love of the theatre and the chance to act. An artist can paint at home, the same with a writer but an actor needs a stage. The major parts would go to older and more established actors. I was offered one of the smaller parts, a good part in a well written play, so I quickly accepted the role. It gave me the chance to work with these experienced and outstanding actors and was a joy. At about the same time I met up with a builder friend who offered me some work. Things were beginning to look up and here I was talking to this beautiful woman, so I invited her to the play which would be opening in less than a week. She smiled and said in her beautiful voice "Yes, I'd love to." I was delighted and kept my fingers crossed she would keep her word.

Even her name sounded beautiful, she was called Honey. The play would be performed in the round, the actors would be in the middle, surrounded by the audience. Once you entered onto the stage you would stay there for the entire play, when it was called for you to sit down, you would be right next to the audience. It was very intimate. The atmosphere was electric. The play received a good reception and there were several well-known faces in the audience, but I'm jumping ahead of myself again! About half an hour before the curtain was about to go up, I was informed that someone was asking for me. I can still see her now standing there with her hair pinned up, she looked beautiful and sounded even more beautiful, those sweet dulcet tones I've never tired of them. After the play we just sat around having a drink and chatting. She was completely at ease. People came up and asked her if she was an actress. Personally I've always thought she would have made a good actress. Like a true gentleman, I offered to walk her to the tube station. On the way there we made small talk and before she departed, I invited her out for a drink later that evening. She said yes. Thus started a beautiful romance, which still endures to this very day, almost forty years later.

Honey is an artist and in her early years she worked for J Walter Thomson, the advertising agency. She has illustrated several children's books and the classics for The Folio Society. She also became an inspirational art teacher. She is still in touch today with some of her students, she taught for many years and even the parents would gravitate towards her, she was very popular. She loved teaching, she put her heart and soul into it. She taught all ages and all sexes even at a very prestigious private boys' school. On reaching retirement age, she was still allowed to go on teaching for several more years, when she did finally retire she was held in such high esteem they named a cup after her. I suppose in some sort of way, she has been immortalised.

Today she is dedicating her time to her own paintings, she's already had a couple of exhibitions and hopefully there's more on the way. She is also building herself a reputation as a children's portrait artist.

I may have already mentioned I was immature for my age, I now believe I am finally catching up with myself, it's taken a long time but I'm getting there. Back then it never occurred to me about settling down and raising a family, I don't think it even entered my head. I had spent my formative years trying to escape my family, not because I didn't love them, of course I loved them and still do, I'd like to think we are a close family if something happens to one of us we all come running. It's just that I wanted and needed my own space.

Eventually I moved in with Honey and her four-year-old son, Luke. It never dawned on me that I now had responsibility and it took me a little time to adjust. I'd like to think I managed it in the end. I liked Luke from the start. Like his mother he was beautiful to look at, amusing and very funny. He was definitely a strong character, always making me laugh and on the odd occasion, angry. He was like a jack in the box, to say he was hyperactive would be an understatement. He certainly wasn't the normal, average, every day, run of the mill kid like those I grew up with. Just ask his friends or people who know him. He is magical, charismatic and he has an edge to him. He is certainly different, maybe that's what they like about him. Maybe that's what makes him so special, like me he was late maturing and like me he became an actor.

I think he was always going to be an actor. His mother thought about going to drama school, but she chose to go to art school instead. Luke has performed in the West End, in films and television. Now he's trying to make is own films, but that takes money, so he's making them on a shoestring. I am also involved in the filming, from soundman, to clapperboard, chauffeur, runner and playing small parts. It's all very difficult without any money, actors will work for nothing but technicians need to be paid. He writes beautiful scripts, he also directs and acts in them. My sister Carol, who lives nearby also helps out when she can. There are times when there is only three of us doing everything and I'm enjoying it.

When I met Honey all those years ago, she was just recovering from an acrimonious divorce but it seemed like perfect timing. We were from completely different backgrounds and as I've already mentioned, times were changing, class barriers were slowly coming down. They're still there, but it's a different world now, better I hope. Before the war it would have been very difficult to break out of your environment, after the war it was a little easier. When I met Honey my life had moved on, I was mixing with people from different backgrounds and the world had opened up for me. I believe once you have moved on you can never go back, if you did it would never be the same. I have wonderful memories of my childhood and the environment I grew up in. I know where I came from and I will never forget it. I was welcomed into Honey's family by her mother and father, who sadly are no longer with us, her brothers, sister, nephews, nieces and her uncles, aunts and cousins. Luke is very close to his cousin David, who now lives in the US, he is also a good friend of mine. They have all become part of my extended family and I know all my family have embraced Honey and Luke and have become part of their extended family.

A Little Nudge

I'd like to think I have been very lucky having my family, my brothers and sisters, my nieces and nephews, my great nieces and nephews and of course Honey and Luke. Judith, one of my nieces, suggested I should write my memoirs "You have all these stories you tell, write it as you tell it," she advised, "tell the stories about the famous and interesting people you have brushed shoulders with." I had thought about it, but lots of people have met and known famous celebrities, there's nothing new there. She was adamant I should write about something, so with a little nudge from her, before my brain became completely atrophied, I decided to write my memoirs.

I wanted to write about the parts of my life my friends knew very little about, but mainly for my family to read. Today my nieces and nephews and their children's lives are far removed from the life our family had when I was growing up. Hopefully I will be able to give them a glimpse into the past, a glimpse into their heritage. We all know that life is not a bed of roses, only some are thornier than others. Maybe they will see that life wasn't all easy back then. Maybe their great grandchildren will look back and think that their lives were not too rosy either, as I know my Gran's life was even thornier than mine. I just happened to be born when the Second World War broke out but I was still there when it was all over, enabling me to play and have fun amongst the damage and wreckage caused by the bombing giving us our adventure playgrounds, without really understanding what really happened. Before the war people were living in those houses.

My mother told me a story about a family, whose name eludes me, who lived in a house only four doors away. The man of the house never used the air raid shelters. Only on this one particular night he decided to take extra blankets to his family who were already in the shelters. During his absence his house was flattened. You might say he was lucky. A lot of people were lucky and a lot of people were unlucky. You can only live in the age you were born in, it's up to you to make the most of it. Somebody once said everybody is equal, but some are more equal than others. When I look back to those days when I was just a kid in Brum, I had no concept of what was going on. Today I'm much older, although still none the wiser.

EPILOGUE

End of the Road

When I go to Birmingham to see my family, I try to arrange with my brother Tony to see a football match, sometimes he brings his grandson Harry and his son-in-law, Stuart. Of course our destination is St. Andrews and The Blues. Often we park the car in Herbert Road. Part of the footprint of Herbert Road is still there and the foot print of the Coventry Road, but everything else has changed, especially Herbert Road.

The Greenway Pub where we sheltered during the bombing in the war has disappeared. The Regent Pub has disappeared and all the shops on that section of the Coventry Road have disappeared too. All the houses in Herbert Road, in fact all the buildings have disappeared, they have been replaced by a new housing estate. On the odd occasion when we have found ourselves walking down Herbert Road, we try to work out where our house once stood and all the various other houses where our friends lived.

All the new houses have small patches of lawn in front of them, with a small fence about twelve inches high sectioning them off, defining the boundaries of each property. It's as if Herbert Road has morphed into the next road Arthur Street. There are also designated play areas, with a basketball area doubling up as a five a side football pitch, open land and a few trees. But there is nobody climbing them, nobody playing there, the place appears deserted. Looking at these modern buildings which have replaced what we thought were almost slum houses, they have somehow missed the mark. If this is a testament to how far we have come in the last fifty years, then we have not journeyed very far. Sometimes when we think things are not working out the way we think they should, we knock it down and start again from scratch, when it might be wiser to keep what we already have and build on it.

Looking back at number 13 it was a good solid house, apart from the kitchen and the outside lavatory. The cellar could have been turned into a utility room plus shower, the kitchen rebuilt and extended upwards, with an extra room and bathroom, maybe even a balcony. Open up the roof and build a dormer, creating a second bedroom with ensuite, endless possibilities. Where was the forward planning? Where was the creativity? What were the architects thinking of? It is true of some architects they don't tell jokes they build them. Maybe the people living in these houses now are going through similar sorts of hardships that we endured. Who's to know? To quote the American humourist, James Ferber "Every man lives a life of quiet desperation." Maybe they are happy with their lot, maybe they have plenty of material things to keep them happy.

I ceased living in that area over fifty years ago. I am stranger there now. London is my home and it has been for the majority of my life. When we stop off on the way to the match to have a drink in one of the very rare pubs that are still standing, I feel like a stranger and walking through the car park of St. Andrews, that once was Kingston Terrace and Cattel Road, feels peculiar. Even the football ground gives me that feeling. Maybe because that too has changed, although for the better with its all seater stadium. Only the pitch remains the same. I always look around searching people's faces before kick-off and at half time when we go for some refreshment. I am half expecting someone to step forward, like a ghost from the past and say "You won't remember me, but aren't you Peter Doherty?" and before he can utter another sentence I would say of course I do and then mention his name.

Maybe then and only then, will I cease feeling like a stranger, in what was literally once my own backyard.

'We are such stuff as dreams are made on,
and our little life is rounded with a sleep.'

William Shakespeare
The Tempest